Quite – *A story of .. ,*

by

Roger H. Panton

Acknowledgements

A big thank you to:
Barry Horner for his civil service fact checking and content suggestions.
Kieron Shaw for his RAF fact checking.
Donna Panton for her overall editing.

Introduction

Dear Reader,

After writing three novels, I've decided to write a true story. A story about myself. Not quite an autobiography, but a memoir, covering some of my real-life experiences as I tried to hide my disappointment from my parents after not being able to continue my full-time education on my arrival in London, from Jamaica, in October 1959.

This was a big thing for me because I had been out of high school for nearly a year waiting to join my parents in London 'next month, next month, next month.' Neither my parents nor I had any inkling that arriving after my 16th birthday would have put me outside the responsibility of the State for compulsory schooling.

In 1959 and for years afterwards, the post-compulsory education system in the UK was not as work friendly as it was in the USA, where one could gain higher-education credits, 'park' them, take time-off for work or other pursuits, and return later to complete one's studies and earn a degree or other academic qualification. In England, the only way forward was to embark on a continuous two-to-four-year course, full-time or part-time, or study by correspondence. If you had a break, you would have had to start all over again.

I engaged in many different pursuits to learn new things and perform at a level I thought worthy of my ability, despite not having paper qualifications to support them. I pushed the boundaries in the hope that what I looked like would not have been a factor in the decisions others would make about me and my capabilities, especially in the military, civil service, and the voluntary activities I got involved with.

When I found myself in a world that demanded certain paper qualifications to progress or to be assigned more-challenging work, I didn't allow myself to be fazed by colleagues who held degrees or other professional qualifications. Instead, I was resolute in my efforts to demonstrate that I was equal to the task. I dared to be different. 'Thinking outside the box' became a habit. I was also fortunate to have had the support of mentors whose insight guided me through some of the difficult stretches along my career path. I was also lucky to have developed a thirst for learning at an early age and my high school in Jamaica instilled in all of us, the belief that we could do anything we wanted to do, if we were given the opportunity. I never lost focus. Even when what I wanted to do, changed along the way, I never considered my past efforts a waste of time. I hoped the skills and knowledge I had gained would be useful again at an appropriate time. I'm convinced that had I been brought up in the UK, I wouldn't have had the drive to disregard the doubters because the society did not provide the Windrush generation children with the positive outlook that's necessary for someone with my determination, yet lacking in academic qualification, to thrive.

An important thing to point out is that because the focus of this book is on my personal journey, it doesn't go into detail about my family life and all the good times I had in raising and developing my family, and the social occasions and holidays we had, or the wide circle of family and friends who played a role in our lives. I'm also happy to say that it was indeed fun being a father and I learnt a lot about myself being a father. Although my two grandsons, Jin and Keiji, call me Grandad, in their early years they really saw me as their grey-bearded playmate. I hope that when the time comes for them to read and fully understand my story, it will provide them with the stimulus to double their efforts in the areas of ambition and determination to succeed in their lives in whatever they undertake as they grow.

I also hope that some of you will take heart from my experiences and never give up. Never give up! Never lose the will to push the boundaries.

Yours truly
Roger H. Panton

CHAPTER ONE
Early Years

One of my earliest memories is rooted in Kingston, Jamaica. My mother said it was just before my third birthday, in April 1946. The story is that I was playing with my 8-year-old brother Lloyd at the house of one of his friends. I must have been bored because Lloyd said that after he refused to take me home, I left without his knowing. What I recall is that a man in khaki shorts dismounted his bicycle, took me by the hand, and asked me where I was going. The next thing I remember is being given milk and crackers by a policeman and hearing the awful scream of a woman who came of out nowhere. She grabbed and hugged me. That's it. That's what I remember of the episode that would lay the foundation of how I would approach life – fearless or, as others might say, reckless at times. It turned out that the cyclist took me to the Rollington Town Police Station, where my Aunt Essie's husband, Sergeant Forbes, was in charge. The station was located at the corner of Giltress Street and Jackson Road, and my aunt and her husband lived next door. Apparently, she was asked to come over and comfort little "lost and found" boy and was shocked to discover that the little boy was me, her nephew. I was a half a mile away from where I'd been playing.

My mother was born Sybil Heron in Costa Rica to Jamaican parents. Her father, John Heron, Jr., was born in Jamaica. His father was born in Scotland and his mother was a black Jamaican. John Jr. was a manager with the United Fruit Company in Port Limon. In Jamaica, he was a pen keeper, raising livestock. Like many Jamaicans in the early 20th century, my grandparents ended up in Costa Rica via Panama. Records show that they were married in Costa Rica in 1913. My grandmother, Ina Heron, nee Lowe, and who we called Mama, returned to Jamaica in 1928, accompanied by her two daughters: my mother, aged 14, and her younger sister Enid. They settled in Kingston and lived a comfortable life. Mama owned and rented a couple of houses and so was able to send her two daughters to a private school. My grandfather did not accompany them and is believed to have died in Costa Rica from typhoid fever. That was never confirmed, and, to this day, the family is unsure of what became of him.

My father, Albert Panton, was a carpenter in Kingston, when he met my mother and her little boy, Lloyd, in 1940. Dad ran an errand for his sister, my Aunt Essie, delivering fabric and collecting the finished dresses my mother made for her. He found all kinds of excuses to visit my mother and they were married in 1941. By 1948, we were a family of four boys and two girls, living in the Kensington district of the parish of Portland, near the extended Panton family. I lived with my paternal grandmother, Christiana Panton (Grannie), in the heart of the district, while the rest of the family lived down by the main road with Dad and Mother Dear (as my mother was known), in a house Dad built. Lloyd remained with Mama in Kingston.

Formal schooling in our area was at the government elementary school for children aged 7 to 15. Younger children had a choice of two private basic schools (kindergartens), situated across the road from each other, where our parents paid for us to be taught by either Miss Blanche or Miss Mary. At age 4, with slate in hand, I learnt to read and write with Miss Mary. She even taught me to say the alphabet backwards, something I delighted in doing in later years with my sons. I had no idea why she taught me to do that. My father told me, years later, that it was because I learnt quickly and was being a bit of a nuisance to the rest of the class. By age 7, I was ready for the elementary school in Manchioneal, two miles from home. Grannie, ever the thoughtful one, decided I should join my family in the house down on the main road, as that would make the walk to school easier for me. I still spent a lot of weekends and holidays with Grannie.

Elementary school was pure fun for me. From age 8 or 9, I began taking part in elocution contests – mainly reciting poems – won a few competitions and went on to represent the school in the annual Portland Arts Festival, winning second prizes. I also had spirited competition for end-of-year class positions from three habitual rivals: Barbara Bryan, Madeline Gordon, and Jeremiah Hall. To this day, Barbara, Madeline, and I still talk about our friendly rivalry. Jerry died a few years ago in a tragic accident in Florida, where he was a university professor. Barbara also became a professor in the United States, and Madeline, a nurse in England.

Mama died in 1953 and my brother Lloyd joined us in Kensington to attend his 5th Form at our local high school, Happy Grove, a boarding and day school, founded in 1898 by the Society of Friends (Quakers) in nearby Hector's River. It has strong links with several American universities where many graduates continue their education. The school colours - purple and gold, reflect the sea of purple and gold blooms in which its iconic church sits. Purple from the vervine plant, and gold of the marigold plant.

At age 11, I took the Happy Grove entrance exam. I remember Grannie saying "Don't send Roger to Happy Grove yet. He's too young." Mother Dear, however, felt that since I had passed the exam, I should go. By then, Lloyd had left Happy Grove in December 1954 after passing his Senior Cambridge Certificate, so I inherited his bicycle to start my high school venture 5 miles or so from home. Lloyd returned to live and work in Kingston, living with my Aunt Enid and working as a journalist at the Daily Gleaner and, later, as a clerk the Halfway Tree tax office.

I believe I settled well into life at Happy Grove, an existence that was made easier because I was Lloyd's little brother. The big boys took care of me. One of them, Frank Salmon, a boarder from Spanish Honduras (now Honduras), lived just a few doors away from Lloyd and my Aunt Enid in Crossroads, Kingston. Of course, I made new friends among my first-year group. Astley Burrowes, a boarder, taught me to play the piano which I still do by ear. That experience led me to buy a piano later in life, and both my sons took piano lessons. One is an accomplished violinist and pianist;

the other studied piano, cello and saxophone before settling on the sax.

The Happy Grove boarders were children whose parents, if not considered rich, were comfortable. Some of these students even had a full driver's license, which was considered a big deal at the time. To me, a day student from the surrounding area, the boarders' life was a privileged one. They outnumbered the day students. They had better access to the library, to the compulsory study periods where classmates learnt from each other and from the older students. They also had a resident Matron. They were able to interact with the teachers outside the classroom, ate their meals together as a family, and had greater opportunities for the sexes to meet and get to know each other well. Their close friendships, therefore, tended to be with each other, but I had a few friends among them. I was a keen sportsman but lacked the ability to be particularly good at anything. I nevertheless made the House Team in athletics, cricket, and football.

I was parted from all but one of my year group at the end of my first year at Happy Grove. The headmaster decided we were both too young to go into Form 2 with the 'big' boys and girls who were just a year or so older than we were. It hurt, especially when I finished at a higher position in the class than some of those who had moved up. At the beginning of my fourth year at Happy Grove, I was joined in Form 3 by my old friends and elementary school classmates, Barbara, and Jerry. Our friendships rekindled. Happy Grove instilled in all of us the confidence that there was nothing we couldn't do. Just give us the training and the opportunity, then watch us. I tried to live up to that.

My father was a member of the Peoples National Party (PNP) and, in 1949, supported Teacher Dillon, headmaster of the Manchioneal elementary school, in his failed bid to oust the East Portland independent MP, Harold Allan. In the local elections, Dad ran for the position of Local Councillor. He was up against Ken Jones, the nearby plantation owner who employed a lot of the menfolk of Kensington. Not surprisingly, Dad lost to Jones. In 1953, Jones ran in a by-election as an independent for the open MP seat of the deceased, by then, Sir Harold Allan, the first Afro-Jamaican Royal Knight. Dad supported the PNP candidate, Adrian Gray, who won. Things were fine for Dad; he was on the winning side. Then Jones ran again in the general election of 1955 under the Jamaican Labour Party banner, and this time he was victorious against Adrian Gray. Losing party members didn't fare too well with government work and, despite Mr. Jones telling Dad that he could be of help to him, Dad decided to take his chances abroad. So, in 1955, he went to England, like so many before him had done. It was also my first year at Happy Grove.

When trying to get her 'British Jamaican' passport to join Dad in England, Mother Dear found she didn't qualify for one because she was a Costa Rican citizen. Her departure was delayed as she renounced her Costa Rican citizenship and became a Jamaican national. The following poem describes how I viewed things in the period between when Dad decided to go and when Mother Dear left to join him with my 2-year-old baby sister Jean Marie, in 1956.

Mother – by R. Huntley Panton (c. 1971)

I remember Mother
You looked so young and sweet
With father by your side
And children at your feet

I remember
How in your rocking chair
You were surrounded by children
Who knew how much you cared
But Father was leaving for England
He was leaving for the 'motherland'

I remember Mother
How you tried not to think
Of a life without father
Though you knew it could be

I remember
How your eyes were filled with tears
When you said goodbye to father
While he tried to hide his fears
It was plain for all to see
He didn't want to leave his family

I remember mother
How you waited lonely days and nights
For those few lines
That would say Father was alright

I remember
When you moved from room to room
Looking tired and weary
As you struggled with the broom
You knew that someday we would understand
Why you had such tired hands

I remember Mother
How you fell asleep over your sewing machine
Then you would wake up, sew again
Only to fall back into a dream
You dreamed of a land far away
And of being with father again one day

I remember Mother
When with a smile on your face once more
You packed to sail away
To Father on that distant shore

I remember
How you fought back your tears
As you told us to be good
And not to fight or swear
Then you assured us
One day we'd be together again
As soon as you could raise the fare

I remember Mother
Though many years have passed since then
And every time I look at you
I know you remember too

I remember Mother
And though mother-time will not turn back
You will get your heart's desire
No longer will you be stranger to your neighbour
No longer will you seek comfort by a fire
You will live again in the land you left behind
Where the people and weather are so often kind

I remember Mother
And mother nature remembers too
For she sits there waiting
To share the past with you

You will hear the drums beat again
The birds and butterflies will be your friends
The moon and stars will light the night for you
To sit and watch the glistening dew
And when you think of the years gone by
You'll turn to Father and you'll both ask, why.

When Mother Dear left for England, we were left in the care of a woman who didn't treat us well. My parents were focused on getting us all up to England as soon as possible. My attendance at school became erratic. Sometimes I walked the 5 miles to school when the person who was supposed to fix my bicycle cannibalised it to repair others. As in elementary school, I was in the boys' choir and represented the school in the Portland Arts Festival. Again, I never got a first prize. Second was not bad, though. I envied the boarders with their compulsory study periods because I had nobody to check that I was doing my homework or help me with any of the lessons. Despite all that, I excelled in Latin, Spanish and English. On the other hand, I didn't fare too well with Mathematics and Chemistry, missing key lessons that taught the mathematical rules and the formulae for chemistry experiments. My friend Pat Chin, who was brilliant in both, did his best to help me. Our friendship continued as we both moved to England and remains the same to this day, here in Jamaica.

Easter 1958 came and went and, of the seven children, only three were still in Jamaica: My sister Barbara was in Kingston with our Aunt Enid; and brother Trevor soon went to another aunt. I would be going to England next month...next month...next month. My attendance became even more erratic. I was told that Mr. Barlow, the headmaster, talked about me and my poor attendance in the morning assembly, one day when I was again absent. December 1958, the end of the academic year, was my last day at Happy Grove. I left for England ten months later, on October 23rd, 1959. I had high hopes of continuing my education.

CHAPTER TWO
London - 1959

When I arrived in London, Dad was a warehouseman with Nestles at Surrey Docks, and Mother Dear, a childminder. With the help of an estate agent who attended the Lewisham Methodist church with them, my parents had managed to buy their own house in Lewisham, hence my delay in joining the family. I thought they'd done very well in their short time in England.

"Mr. Panton…I'm afraid that since your son is no longer of compulsory school age, if you want him to continue studying for his 'O' levels, you'll have to pay for it yourself." My father looked at me with sad eyes. I tried not to look too disappointed and cause him hurt.

"OK. So which school would be the easiest for him to travel to?" my father asked.

"It depends," said the Careers Officer who then asked me about the subjects I'd been studying. He couldn't believe his ears when I mentioned things like, Latin and Spanish. You see, in England in those days, not too many children had access to a school that taught Latin and Spanish. The reality was that with a sister and brother still waiting to come up from Jamaica, paid education was out of the question. Once home, the discussion was about the type of job I would do. Dad felt I should learn a trade as my older brother Deryck was doing in engineering. "There'll always be a need for engineers." Mother Dear felt that, as a high school boy, I should work in an office.

Dad accompanied me to an engineering company in Ladywell, within walking distance from home through the back roads, or a 15-minute bus ride. The owner explained that since I was over 16, I couldn't become an apprentice, but he could take me on as a trainee toolmaker. (One of the characters in my first novel, Mr. Alexander, is, in fact, a toolmaker.) It was agreed, and I started at J Hookey & Son on January 2nd, 1960. To my surprise, next door, at another engineering company, was my former Happy Grove classmate, champion athlete and brilliant cricketer, Clarence "Cushu" Levy. We later played for the Eden Park Cricket Club.

While I was just an average player, Cushu was a star, with many articles being written about him in the South London Press. He was short for a fast bowler, but he had long arms, and was a fearful fast bowler. After a short break, he'd return as an off-break bowler. He batted anywhere in the order, including as opener. He was years too soon for consideration for a County team. They weren't looking at Black players then. Our friendship has continued throughout the years, social media making keeping in touch that much easier. He still lives in London.

I couldn't see myself as a toolmaker doing intricate work because I couldn't read the drawings the skilled craftsmen were working from. Also, nobody had the time to take me under their wing and help me along, as that meant they earned smaller bonus payments. One of the kindest engineers there – Danny Tulhurst – suggested that I attend the South East London Technical College in the evenings and take the Engineering City & Guilds course. Strangely, the other engineers who learnt of Danny's advice said City & Guilds was a waste of time. It should be Ordinary National Certificate or nothing, they said. Another engineer, a Hungarian refugee, told me to "learn to read drawing and you no have to talk to nobody." I reflected on the fact that my brother Deryck seemed to be getting on very well in his apprenticeship and he wasn't going to evening classes. In the end, Deryck and I decided to attend the college together. That's where we met our friend Carl Douglas, of one-hit-wonder fame for his song "Kung Fu Fighting." Carl was studying mechanical engineering, but did a lot of boxing training, and we spent a lot of time in the gym with him when we didn't have classes. In class, I began learning about different types of metals and relearning mathematics. What excited me most, however, was technical drawing. I soon learnt to read some of the drawings used by the engineers at work, and later to understand architectural blueprints.

Around Easter 1961, I had an accident at work and nearly lost a finger. I had failed to adhere to safety rules. Once healed, I decided

I'd had enough of engineering. Mother Dear was happy that I was now looking for an office job. The guys in the workshop were sceptical: "You can't walk out of a factory one day and into an office the next." Some 17 years later, as a civil servant, I went back to the company and tried to get the owner's son, who was then in charge, to participate in a government training scheme that provided placements for young people. Young Hookey seemed genuinely pleased to see me and we had a long chat. The company was not doing well, though, as it was too small to compete with larger enterprises that had moved into automation.

I had a tough time getting an interview for a junior clerk's position and began to believe my former workmates' tale that walking out of a factory and into an office was just not done. So, I renewed my wish to join the army. I'd mentioned this to my parents before. However, because Lloyd had joined and had suffered a nervous breakdown in Germany, my father insisted I could do so only after I reached the age of consent, which was then 21. I was 18. After a few weeks, I got a job at the first interview I attended, as a junior export clerk with Dakin Bros. on Southwark Street. It was a pharmaceutical company and the export arm of Wrights Coal Tar Soap, which did a lot of business in the Middle East and throughout the Commonwealth. The company got most of its leads through the Crown Agents, and my responsibilities included checking invoices, delivering shipping documents to export companies in the City, and collecting dangerous-drug licenses from the Chamber of Commerce. I enrolled in evening classes to learn Spanish at Goldsmiths, Lewisham Way, and started teaching myself to touch type during my lunch breaks. My boss, Mr. Rogers, was impressed with my geographical knowledge and my draft replies to customer enquiries. He was the first older Englishman I came across who didn't have heroic tales about being at the battle front. He had been a firefighter in the war, dealing with the destruction wrought by the bombs dropped on London -- a job I imagined was far more dangerous than the skirmishes that took place on the battlefield. He believed that a direct hit from a bomb would have been better than a festering wound in the mud. A young man called Michael was my mentor (even though I didn't know that word then). Michael suffered hateful anti-Jewish comments from a couple of the clerks. I don't know how he survived there. Together, we often corrected the grammar of our boss's letters, and I think my participation in that editing had something to do with my later transfer to a team that calculated the weight and measurements of crates to arrive at the shipping cost charged to the customer. It was boring and I hadn't yet learnt to keep my feelings to myself, so I was let go after about a year and a half. Despite the ups and downs, I enjoyed my time there, and appreciated the opportunity it gave me to play as a goalkeeper for Wrights Social FC in a South London league on Saturdays.

Still intent on joining the army the following year in April 1964 when I'd be 21, I didn't care too much about what I did. I had several jobs, including working at a laundry for a few months, where I learnt how to sort fabric to avoid the colours running. It came in handy at home in later years, especially with my sons' fancy-coloured clothes. I remember being rewarded with a tip of five pounds by a customer when I handed in a pair of cufflinks that had been left in a shirt. They were of great sentimental value to him. Although it was policy to give such things in to the foreman, I feigned ignorance and went directly to the manager, Mr. Hoare, because the other guys, mostly West Indians on the job claimed that the foreman, who was English, was crooked. Those who worked on Saturdays, cleaning up, said the foreman would come in, take off his shirt, throw it among the dirty ones, and select a clean one to put on and, of course, take home with him.

I was strongly admonished by Mr. Hoare the Tuesday morning after the iconic West Indies cricket team of Frank Worrell, Garfield Sobers, Rohan Kanhai and others famously beat England at the Oval in 1963. I went to the match on the Saturday with a group of friends, and with the excitement of a possible win on Monday, I decided to take the day off from work. (There was no Sunday test match cricket back then.) I was expecting management to have words with me about my absence, because friends told me I was seen in the crowd on television, throwing my raincoat in the air. I did not, however, bargain for the stern telling-off and threat of dismissal for future misdemeanours I got from Mr. Hoare. I walked out. Bad move. Bad move because I think they didn't say nice things about me to prospective employers. Bad move because walking out of my job and living at home meant I didn't qualify for unemployment benefits.

Shortly after that, my parents decided to move from Lewisham to Plumstead, on the London-Kent border. It was going to be some way from my friends. Dad also bought himself a little car and, as I wasn't working, he and Mother Dear paid for my driving lessons. I passed my test on the first attempt. I thought that with my licence I would get a job quickly. It was some time before I landed another job. My brother Deryck, who had a Lambretta scooter, was the next member of the family to pass his driving test.

Despite the setbacks, I had happy times at Sandrock Road with our friends. My home became the central meeting place for us. Life, in general, for us was trouble free. I remember us sitting on the wall of the South East London Technical College in the late night-early morning, listening on a transistor radio to the world heavyweight title fight between Floyd Paterson and Ingemar Johansson. Two policemen on foot patrol stopped by and listened with us for a while before going their way. It also was while we were in Lewisham that a teenage friend, Sitges, who was in the army and with whom we spent the Saturday night at a club, died in a car crash on a German autobahn, just after returning from leave. Sad though that incident was, it didn't dampen my desire to join the army.

I got a temporary packing job in a clothing factory where my brother Trevor worked laying out and cutting material for sewing. Sometime afterwards, our friend Carl's mother bought a Mini and I was their main driver. When she wasn't using the car, I chauffeured Carl and friends on trips out to the airport and back and generally driving around.

Just after Christmas 1963, I had a chat with a childhood friend, Wylie Murchison "Murch" Longmore. He was a member of the Questors Theatre Group, based in Ealing. I became friends with some of his friends and decided to take a chance on trying to get a job in that area for three months until it was time to join the army. I was so naïve that I didn't think of any possibility of being rejected by the army for any reason, including failing the medical test. I had no plan B.

On New Year's Day 1964, I packed my sports bag with essential clothing and other items and just after mid-day, started the walk from Plumstead to where Murch worked in Edgeware Road, aiming to get there an hour or so before he was due to leave for home. Walking to Happy Grove had taught me that you'll arrive. Just start walking. It was winter, but I was well wrapped up. My parents and siblings had no idea of my plan. The journey took me over 3 hours.

I got a job at Perivale Motors in Ealing. I cleaned the showroom cars, the used cars in the yard and the new ones that were bought and ready for collection by their owners. I also delivered and picked up cars from other showrooms around London and the Home Counties. I enjoyed the driving out to the countryside. One weekend, I hired a car from the company to go to a wedding in Gloucester with Murch. The wedding was cancelled, so Murch, being a student of the theatre and Shakespeare, decided we should visit Stratford upon Avon, Shakespeare's birthplace. From there, we decided to go on to Cardiff in Wales. We were surprised to find a border welcome sign in the Welsh language and enjoyed the winding roads and steep inclines and beautiful countryside scenery.

About a week later, an Irish, ex-army man, joined the company as my supervisor. He was given a white coat. I and my Jamaican colleague wondered what tasks he was going to supervise us on.

We found that instead of one of the salesmen giving us the list of cars to prepare, our supervisor would now do that. Instead of our cleaning the cars in the showroom, our supervisor in his white coat would now do that. I thought my driving trips would stop, but they didn't. One day, he asked me why I was doing that job and said he thought something was up. I told him about my plan to join the army. He listened without commenting. The following day, he called me aside and said he thought the army would be a bit too rough for me and suggested I should instead, join the Royal Air Force (RAF). To me, the RAF was all about servicing and flying planes. He explained that there were many options, and I needn't worry as the intelligence test would determine what would be offered to me, and he was sure I'd do well in the test. I thanked him. On or the day after my 21st birthday, 1 April 1964, I entered the RAF Recruiting Office and, after they made a few phones calls behind closed doors, I took a written test. After accepting that I didn't want anything technical (they were reading more into my engineering experience than there was), they mentioned clerical and accounts. I said I wanted to be a driver. They were shocked. One of them said, "No, no laddie. Not with that score." I explained that I wanted to travel and see Britain. (I was smart enough not to say I wanted a job where I would be my own boss, with nobody watching over me as I worked.) The other officer said, "That's alright. They'll sort it out at Swinderby." They then said I'd hear from them in due course.

Back at Perivale Motors, after about three days, I was called into the office by the sales manager, Mr. Simon. He told me the RAF had made enquiries about me and since I would be leaving, they preferred to replace me ASAP. I was sacked on the spot. I returned home to Plumstead. Wylie Longmore, actor-director, married one of the members of the theatre group and lives in Manchester, England. We have a very long friendship to this day.

However much I tried, I couldn't get a new job. I thought it was so, so unfair that because I was joining the military, nobody would employ me. I pestered the RAF guys for an early date. Finally, on

6 July 1964, I signed on for five years; took the Oath at the RAF Information Office in Kingsway, London; boarded the train with others; and went off to the RAF Recruit Training Camp in Swinderby, Lincolnshire. I was now Airman Panton.

CHAPTER THREE
RAF – UK

I enjoyed my time at Swinderby, making friends with guys from all over Britain, the Caribbean and India. I learnt about aspects of British life that I had hitherto been shielded from. For example, a couple of the guys who lived on farms talked openly about having sex with their sisters. It didn't seem to unsettle the others except for the Caribbean contingent. There was a guy nicknamed Miner because he was previously a miner. The conditions under which he said he had worked didn't seem real to me. Some of the guys seemed afraid of water. Despite having showers at their disposal, they would wash their face, armpits, and feet in the wash basins. We from the Caribbean, even if we didn't have showers at home, were accustomed to running water. In London, my brothers, friends, and I went to the public baths in New Cross or Lewisham to have showers. Forsaking the showers and doing what those guys did was indeed a shock to us.

I also came face to face with crude racism for the first time. A couple of the guys would make racist comments softly, out of earshot of others. They were, however, in the minority. The West Indian group consisted of guys like Basil Inverary, a cool, calm giant of a fellow from Guyana. Asquith Wright from Jamaica. He was ambitious and wanted to become an engineer. A former Kenya Colonial Policeman, Stuart McKay, a nice guy, received the prize for Best Recruit. After the Passing Out Parade, Sergeant. Green, whose stature was that of a jockey and who looked too old to be still in the services, and who oversaw our day-to-day training, took me aside and told me I had been beaten to the prize by the best recruit they'd had for some time. True or not, I was pleased to hear it. A few years later, Stuart became a Commissioned Officer in the RAF Police.

On arriving at the RAF Driver's Training School in Newton, Lancashire, I was full of confidence when I found the rest of the recruits consisted of folks who didn't yet have a driver's licence. I foolishly saw myself as being in training for a shorter time than they. We attended classes on the road code, minor vehicle servicing, the paperwork required for taking a vehicle on the road, and accident reporting; and we were tested on these things. The instructors were a mix of civilians and RAF personnel. There seemed a competition between them as to who had the best-looking female recruit. I had a civilian instructor. Our first day out, we were taken to a disused airfield where we drove around in three-ton trucks without bumping into each other. On the way back from our first morning out driving, I casually asked my instructor when I could expect to go on the road. "Not for another week," he said. I said nothing, but, feigning ignorance, decided to go straight to the top with my complaint. I knocked on the door of the Warrant Officer, the most senior non-commissioned officer. He held it ajar, looked at me questioningly before asking me what I wanted. I told him that although I already held a driver's licence, my instructor had told me I would have to drive around the airfield for another week before I could go out on the road and I didn't think it was fair. He told me that I needed to see Sergeant Orme with such complaints. I apologized and left.

Sergeant Orme was my instructor that afternoon. We spent about five minutes on the airfield before he told me to head out onto the road. He was incredibly quiet, talking only to give me instructions: turn left; turn right; use your mirrors; watch your speed; park. After driving up and down the road, he told me to stop, then he took over. We returned to camp. He made no comment about my driving. Later, my fellow recruits said I had been foolish to go straight to the Warrant Officer and feared that I might be kept on the airfield longer because of it. The next morning, a smiling Sergeant Orme told me that he would be my instructor.

I soon learnt that Sergeant Orme was an amateur rally driver and he really enjoyed driving, so much so that the driving was shared about 50-50 between us. He was inclined to commentaries like this: "See how the shadows of the trees are lying on the road? We know there are no obstacles immediately around the bend otherwise we would see their shadows…On right hand bends, go out left and drive into the corner. On left hand bends, stay as close as you can to the white line and drive into the corner. Always try to drive around corners. Slow down before and keep the driving wheels working through the turn...I know a farm gate is up ahead on my left and it is a blind exit. Touch the horn. Let them know you are there. That's the only purpose of the horn, to let drivers and pedestrians know you're there…Watch your speed, always." We had lots of fun as he made fun of my attempts to match his smooth directives. I was grateful for how he taught me, especially when I realised that such commentary was not an aspect of the training course.

Soon after finishing my driver's training, we were notified that the Driving School would be relocated from Weeton to St. Athan in South Wales. As no postings were being done for the time being, we were kept busy packing equipment and generally preparing for the move. Come the day of the move, as the vehicles were positioned to leave in a convoy and just before the order to board was given, the Warrant Officer called me, gave me the paperwork and keys of one of the cars and said: "Panton, you're driving down to St. Athan."

It was for me quite an experience and the journey reminded me of my trip to Wales earlier in the year. The hills and valleys were breath-taking. I saw beautiful 'picture postcard' thatched cottages and names of places like Ross-on-Wye. After a brief stay at St. Athan, I was given a posting to RAF Cardington in Bedfordshire. I took my Spanish book with me.

RAF Cardington is a station with a lot of history. Located just south of Bedford, it is immediately identifiable by its two outsized hangars. It was the home of the airships. When I arrived, I was introduced to something incredible that I'd never heard of before. I was joining a team that would inflate a balloon with 45,000 cubic feet of highly inflammable hydrogen gas. Being lighter than air, it would drift away if not tethered to the ground or to a strong structure, in this case a 10-ton lorry. Attached to the balloon and hanging by a series of cables, was a cradle, a box that could hold four paratroopers and a despatcher. It had a door out of which the paratroopers would jump 800 feet and float to the ground. The balloon also had stabilizers and an aircraft-like rudder that kept the nose turned into the wind. It was essential for the paratroopers to drift away from the truck below that held a winch that controlled the cables to the cradle. I was a winch operator. I would release the winch at a controlled slow speed, so as not to make the paratroopers seasick. After they jumped, I would haul the cradle back in for the next batch of jumpers. It was an efficient way of getting paratroopers to learn to jump and fall correctly. Once trained, they would repeat the exercise at least once during the year to maintain their parachute wings. The Territorial Army paratroopers were our best 'customers' as we travelled nationwide to places like Catterick, the Sunderland Flying Club (now Nissan), and Scotland.

I was soon sent on a work study project – to research how to reduce the time parachutes take to dry. There were four of us: A Flight Lieutenant, a Flight Sergeant, an airman who made tea and did other odd jobs, and me, the winch operator. The main equipment was a parachute that was kept open with wires as it would be while falling; heat blowers; a note pad; and a stopwatch. We spent days working on different ideas. On day two, sitting in my seat on the winch, I had an idea that I thought might assist the project and I mentioned it to the Fight Lieutenant. He didn't quite understand what I was trying to say so he called me to come and explain. After asking a few questions he said it wouldn't work because of something relating to the strength of the blower, the size of the room, and the number of parachutes they wanted to dry at any one time. He thanked me for thinking about it rather than just sitting there operating the winch. I was later admonished by the Flight Sergeant for speaking direct to the Flight Lieutenant. Rightly or wrongly, I thought he was just jealous that I dared to speak up and that the Flight Lieutenant listened.

Soon after arriving at Cardington, I became friends with some Caribbean guys who were already there. They briefed me on the dating scene which mostly involved the Caribbean nurses at the Bedford General Hospital. Competition was tough with the Black Americans from the US Signals base at nearby Chicksands. Many of them had cars and we didn't. (This also features in my book - Mr. Alexander.) They could also offer the prospect of life in the USA, which was quite something then. Some of the nurses did marry the US guys. Not long after arriving there, I phoned the nurses' residence and asked to speak to one of the Caribbean nurses. I did this from time to time, chatting with whoever came on the phone and was friendly and talkative. In those conversations, we would talk about the islands we hailed from and what we hoped to achieve in England, and it wasn't too long before a young lady from Nevis caught my attention.

After a year's service, I was promoted to Senior Aircraftman and was able to drive a 10-ton truck. On my first trip to Arbroath in Scotland, I came face to face with the reality that Scotland was truly a different country. The Sunday papers carried the Scottish football results first and the main articles were about the Scottish Clubs. The English results were less conspicuous. They also had their own Scottish Bank Notes. This might be nothing to many of you. However, to me, a Jamaican who before coming to Britain viewed every native English-speaking European as English, and who had never been to Scotland before, it was a revelation. Wales hadn't gone to the extent of having their own banknotes, even though their welcome at the border was in Welsh.

I wasn't a smoker or drinker and that put me in the category of those who would have fewer friends. I was taught to play basketball by a Trini friend, Noel Viera, and ended up playing a couple of games on his Trini team, The Hummingbirds. One opposing team was the Metropolitan Police. They and the Central London YMCA fielded strong teams. I tried getting onto the Cardington football team as a goalkeeper but was kept out by Noel and the No.1 pick, "Rolly Polly" Everard, who was nearly 40-years old, brilliant, and always in the right place to make a save look easy. One of our cooks, a Welshman, Sergeant Doug Veasy, asked if I'd like to have a go at rugby. The only rugby I'd ever seen was on television, and boy was it rough and nasty! I declined. Sergeant Veasy came back the next day and explained that what I saw on TV was rugby league and that rugby union had different rules that made the game safer. "Tell you what," he said, "come and train with me three evenings next week and at the end of it, you decide. How's that?" What a reasonable man, I thought to myself. We had a deal. The training sessions lasted about two hours each and consisted of running in between poles that would be put closer together as the session went along. Then it was the simple matter of catching the ball from on high and passing it to each other on the run. This was followed by picking up the ball on the run, learning to tackle and to evade tackles, and shielding the ball when on the ground. I really enjoyed the training and was ready for my first game as full back because he felt I had "safe" hands. The last thing he said to me before kick-off was, "Remember, just kick it into touch if you feel uncomfortable about a situation."

I had a memorable first game, memorable for good and bad reasons. First, I ran with the ball too often instead of kicking it into touch, as per Doug's advice. I was therefore tackled with the ball. On the other hand, I proved to be what they described as a fearless tackler, having been properly taught by Sgt. Veasy. In the end, I scored the winning try when I went on a run instead of passing the ball. That was the beginning of what turned out to be a real passion for me.

I played cricket as well. I was 6 feet 1 inch tall with long legs and long arms. I became a much-improved fast bowler because of a simple tip a Scotsman, Dennis Halpin gave me. He told me to shorten my long runup and follow through after delivering the ball. The shorter runup and follow through gave me more control and I was just as fast but more accurate with my outswingers. I was surprised that such a simple adjustment was so effective. I got more wickets because of it.

Still, at Cardington, my Warrant Officer (Crossman, I think was his name), called me into his office one day and told me to report to RAF Abingdon the coming Friday evening to start training as a high jumper the next weekend. He explained that because of the way I jumped at a basketball tournament, the Physical Training Officer believed he could turn me into a high jumper.

It was an indoors training session under the control of John Le Muserier, the then Amateur Athletic Association (AAA) National Coach. Le Muserier's pride and joy, Mary Rand, had won the Olympics long jump title the previous year, 1964. I spent most of the Saturday morning session doing stretching exercises akin to being a ballet dancer. I was then shown the straddle technique which was the current style of jumping: right leg fully extended upwards while the left remained in contact with the ground, then lift off and roll over the bar. The leg extension was difficult to achieve. I thought it was too much to ask of me at age 22. It was much too late in life to achieve any real height. Too late to start that sort of nonsense, I thought. Furthermore, it was one of those events that appeared monotonous and not attractive to the spectators. I wasn't surprised nobody wanted to do it. Despite all that, by Sunday lunchtime I was able to jump about 5 feet 6 inches and was immediately placed on the Transport Command team. (Poor by today's standard, I'm sure.) I took part in competitions all over the south of England against RAF bases and civilian clubs, including Brighton Athletics Club and a touring Swedish team. My high jumping which had improved was no match for the Swedes, though.

I joined the Bedford and County Athletics Club. Ian Green who later sprinted for Britain and Joe Bugner, the boxer, were there at the time. Joe was the England Youth discus champion. It was there that I found that I could run a bit and I tried the triple jump as well. Soon I was running one of the sprint relays legs, doing the high jump and the triple jump. I was not brilliant at any of them. Still, I was good for points which was the important thing in many of the competitions at the club and the RAF. In preparing to take a jump, one of our officials would come over to the high jump pit and say to me: "After this jump, pop over to the triple jump and just put a decent jump in. We need the points." Not the best preparation for a high jump competition. But that's the military for you. Despite all that, I must say that I loved the competitions and the travelling associated with them. It beat being at work. I also got many free days, being allowed time off from work before a competition, the day of the competition, and sometimes at least the morning after the competition. An example of the latter is when I went to Brighton Athletics Club. I had the Tuesday afternoon off, so I stayed with my parents in London the Tuesday night; travelled by train to be in Brighton the Wednesday afternoon; competed, then stayed again at home the Wednesday night; was back to camp by mid-morning by train on Thursday, then told to report to work Friday morning.

In November 1965, Ian Smith, Prime Minister of Rhodesia (now Zimbabwe), declared his country's independence from Britain. Most of the English guys were vociferous in their stance that they would rather go to prison than fight against their own white folks in Rhodesia. They mirrored Harold Wilson's government's position of not acting against the Smith regime for its blatant mutiny against the Queen's rule and its brutal treatment of the

African population. It was an uncomfortable time for us Black airmen as, not long afterwards, some of the very airmen were volunteering to go to Aden to help in the RAF withdrawal from that country.

I volunteered to be an usher at the 1966 Wimbledon Tennis Tournament but didn't receive a response. One day, my Warrant Officer called me into his office. He offered me a cup of tea. I thought it was unusual. He got straight to the point. "Panton," he said, "They do want you at Wimbledon and I want you here on our cricket team. (I noted the personal "I"). I'd really appreciate it if you declined their invitation." He then leaned forward and whispered, "I can also guarantee you that you'll never set foot in Aden." That last statement was nice to hear but a little troubling, because up to then, all postings to Aden for the withdrawal were volunteers. I'd nevertheless learnt that these Warrant Officers, the highest of the non-commissioned ranks, wielded great power. I didn't go to Wimbledon or Aden.

One day I got a surprise invitation from the football team manager – Sergeant Latham – to play in his five-a-side football team trials. It was going to be a fast and furious training session from which he was going to select two teams to enter an East Anglia knockout competition. I knew the only way I could get into the team was as goalkeeper, and that would only be if Everard and Noel weren't available. I just didn't have the ball-control skills for other positions. During the trial, however, I found I was fitter than most and had a powerful and reasonably accurate blast in front of goal. I was surprised to be selected to play on Team A. The regular footballers weren't happy with the decision. Come the day of the competition, Sergeant Latham didn't travel with us and Sergeant Ross, one of the regular players was in charge. He relegated me to the B team. Team A was knocked out in the first round, but then played in the Plate competition for all first-round losers. We, Team B, played three games before being knocked out. Team A played more games than we did because they did very well in the Plate competition before being knocked out. I don't know what was said between Sergeant Ross and Sergeant Latham, but Sergeant Latham later apologized to me for being kicked off Team A, even though I hadn't made a complaint. I'd decided early on to choose the battles I'd fight. Not being on team A wasn't one of them.

The International Four Days Marches Nijmegen (Internationale Vierdaagse Afstandsmarsen Nijmegen) is the largest multiple marching events in the world, according to Wikipedia. It takes place every year in Nijmegen, Netherlands in mid-July. It averages 40 kilometres per day over four consecutive days. Military participants must march in formation and in uniform while carrying at least 10 kg of dry weight each day. This difficult 160 km march takes place in and around the city. In the summer of 1966, I was among those who volunteered to train for the March. We had a three-day test in the UK with backpack, and anyone who failed to finish wouldn't make the trip. Sergeant Veasy was among those of us who qualified. A few days before we were scheduled to play a cricket cup semi-final in East Anglia, Sergeant Veasy told us that the cup final was scheduled for when we would be in Holland. He smiled, shrugged his shoulders, and walked away. Not one of us, to my knowledge, said a word to each other about it, but we lost the semi-final match because of some sloppy fielding and careless batting. Our Warrant Officer was furious over the loss. We went on our one-week trip to Holland.

We flew to RAF Laarbruch in Germany and travelled by coach to Nijmegen. I was excited. I'd joined the military for travel. We were all in good spirits. There were troops from all over the world. Even the London Metropolitan Police had a team. The march was more difficult than we thought. The first day was a warm-up of about 35 kilometres, so we had 5Ks to make up. The second was about 40. Still 5Ks to make up. The 3rd day was a killer of just over 50Ks, giving us an easier 4th day. We sang as we marched along, being soaked to the skin in rainfall then drying out only to be soaked again. We had shots of schnaps at roadside bars. We copied marching songs from the American teams. The beautiful, shapely Israeli female soldiers in their yellow blouses were the darlings of all the guys. We marched and sang for them as well. I was enjoying it all. The Dutch folks lined the roads and cheered us on. I made friends with a young lady, Tilli, who I met on day 2. She was waiting for me on days 3 and 4 and walked along chatting with me for about half an hour each day. The Dutch, to me, seemed to have a cruel sense of humour on day 4. We came around a bend and were told that the church we could see in the distance was where the finishing line was. A sudden burst of energy was transferred to our leg muscles and our voice boxes. Those of us nursing blisters could feel them no more. Then, after a half an hour or so, we didn't seem to be getting any closer. "Don't look at the church lads," shouted Sgt Veasey. "Just keep it going." And so, we kept it going, walking slower than before, the blistering feet hurting again, until sometime much later, we hobbled to the finish line. We'd done it.

Near the end of summer 1967, I went running around the airfield in the mornings with a young man whose father was Polish and an officer at a nearby RAF station. The family lived in married quarters at Hullavington. I believe the young man was on summer holiday from university. Soon, his sister started joining us near the end of our runs, and we would chat while her brother drifted away from us. I was later invited to their home one afternoon for tea. Both her brother and mother found reasons to leave us alone. I was scared that sort of thing could end up getting too serious, as she was not yet 18, and I decided it wasn't a good idea for us to continue seeing each other.

Soon afterwards, in September, I was on alert for an overseas posting. I was hoping to get to Germany and started learning German using the Linguaphone method. Then the news came: I was going to Cyprus. First, I would be assigned to 112 Squadron, an anti-aircraft missile Squadron I'd never heard of. I was the only black airman there and I lived at nearby RAF Conningsby. My stay there was short as they were already packing up in preparation to relocate to RAF Episkopi. In October, a Caledonian Airways plane left the RAF Conningsby airfield with us, bound for Cyprus. They told me it was unusual for an airline, rather than the RAF, to make such a trip.

CHAPTER FOUR
RAF – Cyprus

Cyprus is a strategic island in the eastern Mediterranean, at the crossroads of Africa, Asia, and Europe. Although much closer to Turkey, it was ruled then, by the Greeks, although the population was made up of largely of Greeks and Turks. British Forces have been on the island for many years, the UK having what they called "Sovereign Bases," outside the jurisdiction of the Cyprus government. In addition, there was a contingent of UN soldiers to keep the peace between the two communities. The Episkopi base, at the time, housed soldiers, and airmen.

I barely slept that first night in Cyprus, as I spent most of the night listening to the crickets, frogs and whatever else chose to enter or leave the noisy chorus. I watched the stars move around the dark sky, interrupted by moving flickers of aircraft lights that interfered with their display. I was transfixed. It had been 8 years since I had experienced the tropical heat and night-time sounds of Jamaica, and I realized for the first time the beauty of what I'd left behind.

No.112 Squadron was a heap of boxes and machinery that quickly turned into an operational anti-aircraft missile site. We were first located on the edge of the Episkopi camp before moving to Paramali, a mile or so away from the main camp. Many of the Squadron's Technicians were young corporals and sergeants. They walked tall with chests puffed out with a "we are the bright boys," persona. They didn't mix much with the rest of the folks on the Station that include army and other RAF personnel and were not at all liked by them. The Squadron therefore became the team to beat in sports competitions. We however had a good team in all the regular sports and therefore no pushover.

I had subscribed to Time Magazine from I was in the UK and I continued to receive my copy every fortnight from Holland. Some of the Squadron guys viewed me suspiciously because of that. It was like, "What is he trying to say or to prove?" I guess being a driver, I shouldn't have had an interest in the subjects carried by such a publication.

I became friends with many of the Caribbean soldiers who were from all the islands. They warned me to stay away from the local young ladies because the men, both Greek and Turkish Cypriots, were fierce defenders of their women folk, especially when it came to the Black boys. In the Mess (dining room), we, the Caribbean soldiers and airmen, sat at a long table together. We were noted for our laughter. Only newcomers were troubled by it. Sometimes, usually at weekends, we never left the mess after our mid-day meal and some of the white guys didn't like that the Turkish catering staff would clean up around us and let us stay till tea-time. If folks only knew the types of things that caused us to roar with laughter sometimes. Here's one. Our triple jump champion, Sam, a tall Nigerian, considered himself a ladies' man. Unfortunately, he couldn't cope well with rejections. One lunchtime, one of the beautiful WAFs (Women's Royal Air Force) who had rejected his advances was walking out of the mess. She had just approached where we were sitting, close to the exit, head held proudly high, not looking at anyone. Sam said to us in a slow, exaggerated, broad Nigerian accent: "I would like to trow 'er up against de wall and charge!" I leave you to imagine the uproar that emanated from our table. We were virile, sometimes-frustrated young men away from home.

As part of our welcome briefing was a chat by the Chaplain. He made a point of emphasizing that if ever we felt pressure from anything or anyone, we shouldn't hesitate to come to see him.

"Don't let things fester," he said. "I'm here for you. Come and talk to me." In the weeks that followed, he seemed to just wander about the place not appearing to be doing anything. One day, I was thinking about what he had said, and I decided I'd go and have a chat with him and find out exactly what he did. I knocked on his door.

"Oh…Did I forget an appointment?" he asked.

"No sir," I replied. "I thought you said we could just pop in to see you."

"Well, never mind. Have a seat. You're Panton, aren't you? From 112 Squadron?"

"Yes Sir."

"Yes, Father, is fine."

It wasn't strange that he knew me because most of the folks knew me because of my sporting activities. I told him I had no issues but just wanted to understand his role and the sort of things he would deal with. He didn't seem convinced, but he told me about others he'd dealt with who had bereavement at home, and relationship problems. He then asked me if I had left a girlfriend in the UK. (If I had a wife, he'd have known.) I told him "female friends, yes…but no girlfriend, so to speak." Not sure he believed me. We had a little chit-chat and I left. I'm sure he thought he'd be seeing me again for the real reason he thought I was there. A few days later, he was dining with friends in a Limassol restaurant when I entered with Irene, a WAF. He took a double take and nearly chocked when he recognized us. To this day I don't know why he reacted in that way. I never went back to see him, but we nodded with a little smile whenever we came across each other.

My sporting efforts travelled with me from the UK and I was soon representing Episkopi in athletics, cricket, basketball, and rugby. The latter an average of twice a week. Bruises, aches, and pains hardly had time to recover before I was back on the field. I played my first game of rugby at age 21 and wished I had done so earlier. I was moved from fullback and played more regularly on the wing, then centre, one of the star positions among the backs. Although I was a decent centre, I lacked the fast thinking necessary to be a good one. That speed of thought comes with experience that I didn't have. Still, I was invited to play on the teams from which the RAF Cyprus squad was chosen but I wasn't selected. That I was invited was a good feeling. They had some really good players out there, including a couple of star centres who I was told played for the top-ranked London Hospitals. They were doctors Potts and Pryor, getting on a bit in years. My pride was bruised when I had to move from the centre to the wing to accommodate them. The toughest competitions I personally faced were against the Fijians in the army's 47th Dragoon Guards. They were hard-hitting and fearsome runners with the ball. My most satisfying games were in 1969 when I scored the only two tries to win the semi-finals of our cup competition and followed it up with the only try in the finals, which won us the Cup. We were the Griffons, from RAF Episkopi.

The Episkopi PT team organized a skiing trip to the Troodos Mountains (Cyprus has a skiing season, though not a long one.) Free instruction was provided by an Austrian Army ski instructor. And so, it was, that I learnt to ski.

Our sports ground had the wonderful name of Happy Valley. I got better at cricket and was a permanent member of the Squadron and Station teams. Our competitors were much stronger than in the UK and I was overshadowed many times by others, especially the Sri Lankan and Caribbean players. One night, after heavy rainfall, Happy Valley was destroyed by flood water that seemed to deposit the mountainside on it. I decided to spend my time in the gym and soon found myself being the sparring partner of a welterweight who had an up-coming fight against a southpaw. Not having a southpaw to help him prepare, I agreed to switch my normal stance and become his southpaw sparring partner. Just days before the fight however, I had to switch back to my natural stance as I weas asked to become a fighter against an army light-heavyweight. He'd had only four fights, they told me, and his opponent was injured. I was 6 feet 1 and weighed 174 pounds – a light heavyweight. I agreed.

Bombardier Brown was shorter than me and stocky, and about the same weight as me. When the bell rang for the first round, it was, for me, a lonely and scary moment. This guy had fought four times before. Still, I told myself, the referee would protect me in the three rounds to come. In the first round, I tried to keep Brown at a distance with jabs as the physical training instructor had instructed me. In the middle of round two, after a flurry of punches between us at close range, I dropped Brown twice and he began to bleed from the nose. I couldn't cope with the blood being sprayed on me every time he breathed out, so I spent the rest of the round and the third, staying away from him, but peppering him with jabs, as I had done in the first. I won the fight on points.

I went to Malta in 1968 and 1969 with the RAF Cyprus athletics team. Our opponents were Combined Services Malta (Army, Navy and RAF), and the Malta National Team. I'd become a 440-yards runner by then with a personal best of 51.1 seconds on a cinder track. Given that I wasn't an athletics specialist with the appropriate training for the event, I was happy with that time because I felt that if I had concentrated on athletics, I could have lowered it to 48 or 49 seconds. I competed in the high jump, triple jump, 440 yards and relay. Again, the high jump was interrupted by me having to go over to the triple jump pit and return to the high jump. We won the competition on both occasions.

In April 1969, I became a qualified mobile crane operator. A short time afterwards, I was promoted from Senior Aircraftman to Corporal, months earlier than drivers would normally be considered for promotion. On the day I got my stripes, the Station Warrant Officer briefed all of us newly promoted on what would happen when we were called in by the Station Commander for a congratulatory pep talk. When it was my turn, Group Captain Clause just smiled, shook my hand, said congrats and added that he was sure we would run into each other soon in Happy Valley. The

Station Warrant Officer didn't seem at all pleased with the apparent casualness between the Group Captain and me. He didn't know that when I went for my runs early mornings down at Happy Valley, I often met the Group Captain, who was also out, horse-riding. Occasionally he'd stop and have a chat with me. It never affected my showing him the respect due.

It's rare to be kept in the same post upon promotion. However, I took over the Corporal driver position on the Squadron. My predecessor had been sent to RAF El Adem in Libya, and he sent word back that they were expecting a Corporal Panton. Somebody had fixed it for me.

Corporal Mike Bull was the Squadron Mechanic. Whenever there were two NCOs (non-commissioned officers) of equal rank in the MT (Mechanical Transport) Section, the driver would be the one in charge. The technicians weren't pleased with that because, although the Squadron had specialist vehicles for transporting the missiles, I was in charge of the vehicle movements. If they wanted the use of a car or minibus, they had to seek my authorization. Some of them just couldn't bring themselves to ask my permission. On a few occasions they would ask Mike, but he'd only do it if I wasn't around. Some even went directly to my boss, Flight Lieutenant Duncan, only to be referred to me. Mike was a decent fellow. He had more years than me in the RAF and made corporal before me. He lost no time in briefing me on the paperwork that was specific to the Section. Years later, I learned he'd gained a commission and had become a Flight Lieutenant. I was pleased to hear that.

Flight Sergeant Guy was one of the senior NCOs who didn't feel comfortable asking me about using a vehicle, especially when I'd ask a question or two to see if I could coordinate it with other trips. One evening, he came face to face with me in an aisle in the library and nearly had a heart attack. He seriously asked me what I was doing there. After a little chat, he decided to introduce me to the writings of George Bernard Shaw. He selected "Pygmalion," on which the films, My Fair Lady, and some say, Pretty Woman, are based. When I began reading it, it overpowered me. The introduction was a short story on its own. Every now and then, he delighted in asking me how I was getting on with it. He seemed surprised when I was honest with him that it would take me two or three readings to make sense of it, and was even more surprised when, months later, I told him I'd read it and then had a little discussion with him about it. He had clearly suggested it to me as a laugh, not expecting me to read it. By his action, he gave me the opportunity to at least know who George Bernard Shaw was, and be introduced to his writing. Flight Sergeant Guy's attitude to me became a bit more pleasant after that.

Kieron Shaw was one of the clerks on the Squadron. We became friends early on. When his father, a serving RAF officer, died suddenly in the UK, Kieron had to return at short notice. He was, like me, close to the end of his tour in Cyprus, so he went home early. He left his personal stuff with me to pass on to the RAF folks to ship back to him, and the guys on the Squadron couldn't understand why he chose me and not one of them. They had no idea about friendships.

My stay in Cyprus, from 1967 to 1970, was during the period when there were skirmishes between the Turkish Cypriots and the Greek Cypriots. The rough stuff took place before and after I was there. The UN Charter for peacekeeping operations was renewed every six months. The Cypriots made a lot of money from the troops being there. Many homes were built specifically for rental to the married troops and airmen. Bars, restaurants, and a host of commercial operations benefitted from the military presence. Because of that, a few weeks before the Charter came up for discussion, there'd be a harmless explosion at a water pump or some other location to get the UN to renew operations for another six months. After the British Press published a story about a bomb going off in the Cypriot capital of Limassol, under a British Forces school bus, minutes after it dropped of its load of school children, my parents thought I was facing the sort of danger prevalent in Vietnam at the time. The truth was that the driver of the bus chose to pop into a bar instead of driving directly back to camp after dropping the students off. It was time for the UN Charter to be reviewed, and someone put a little explosive device in a cigarette packet under the bus. It caused superficial damage but, of course, it had the desired effect. The UN Charter was renewed as usual.

At different times, I dated a couple of the WAFs. We mostly went to a restaurant or clubbing at the Calypso Club in Limassol, owned by a Jamaican, a former soldier. That's where I had another scary moment, nearly wetting myself. Some new troops in uniform were in town. I didn't know who they were or where they had previously been posted. A group of about five of them were at the club. One guy didn't like the fact that I was dancing with a girl who I knew well, after she'd refused to dance with him. He made his disgust known by gesticulating to me. I ignored him. When the music ended, he poked me in my chest and said, "If you want a fight come outside." I punched him full on the chin and he fell, dragging me down with him. The two Bajan boys who were nearby, ran out of the club leaving my army buddy Steve Quashi from Trinidad and me as the only Black squaddies. Steve warned the others not to get involved. As soon as I got to my feet, I felt myself being held from behind with my arms trapped by my side. I prepared my body for a good beating. Luckily, one of the soldiers held his colleague in a similar fashion, stopping the fight. To this day, I have no idea why I reacted so quickly and so fiercely. It was like an out-of-body experience. That wasn't me. My brothers and friends back in the UK would have found my reaction hard to believe.

On another occasion, I had a moment of sheer madness. I feel cold sometimes when I think of it. There was a black WAF who worked in the clinic. One day, a soldier known to us for his racist comments whenever he smelt alcohol, was reported to have made an insulting and racist comment to our nurse friend. I and a couple of the

Caribbean guys went looking for him. Luckily, we didn't find him. We would all have been in serious trouble. The things we do as young men!

My sister Barbara decided to get married in October 1968, and I flew back to Britain for it. I was best man. She was marrying Ancel, a friend of mine before he became her friend. He'd quit the army because he was lovesick for her. It was nice being back and meeting up with family and friends. Since I'd been in Cyprus, both my brothers, Deryck and Trevor, had moved to the US. Deryck's engineering apprenticeship in London had worked out well for him. General Electrics had come to Britain to recruit engineers for its aircraft factory in Lynn, Massachusetts. The terms of the recruitment included the engineers being able to take their families with them. They would also be able to remain and work for any employer in the US after their contract period ended. Deryck, who had married in 1963, was recruited and went first, to sort out suitable accommodation for his family. Trevor followed later, escorting Deryck's wife, son, and daughter. Both my brothers eventually made the US their home, with Trevor eventually owning a ladies-wear factory.

CHAPTER FIVE
RAF - Back in the UK

The end of my tour of duty in Cyprus coincided with my sister Beverley getting married in April 1970. After the wedding, I went to the US for a month. It was great meeting up with my brothers Deryck and Trevor again, plus the many schoolmates who had made New York their home. They told me they expected to see me at the end of my RAF service, emphasizing that as military veteran I'd have no problem getting a visa and permanent stay if I wanted it.

I was like a little child, excited, when I had to take my trip to Boston, Massachusetts, alone, to see Deryck. I'd seen the Greyhound buses in films, and I was going to enjoy a ride in one. It wasn't as luxurious as I'd imagined, but it was a nice ride. I had a pleasant encounter with a bearded white guy who asked me how long I'd been in the US. When I said, "a fortnight," he burst out laughing, saying out loud, "I haven't heard that word since I read Shakespeare." Others joined in the laughter, even though I wasn't sure they'd heard all the exchange.

Deryck lived in Lynn, about 15 miles outside Boston. I spent a few hours one day looking around Boston. It was a bit like Europe, with curving streets. While admiring a European-style building, I asked a passer-by what the building was.
"Yes…it is the courthouse, and your entrance is around the side," he said, pointing out the direction. I wanted him to see my look of surprise at his response, but his back was towards me as he headed towards the entrance at the front of the building.

While I was in New York, the "Hard Hats" (construction workers), went on an assault against Kent State University students who were demonstrating against the Vietnam war and President Nixon's announcement of the invasion of Cambodia. It was horrific. I told myself that living in an environment where people could get away with assaulting young people the way the Hard Hats did wasn't for me. I doubted I'd ever live in the US. I didn't think, with my personality, I'd survive there. I later had a memorable visit with my brother Trevor to the Apollo Theatre in New York City, on Amateur Night. Singers would come onstage and do their thing and were booed off or applauded as the audience saw fit. The host was the "Iceman," R&B singer Jerry Butler. He was very cool. Guest artistes were Irma Franklin, The Ojays, and Los Chicanos, – a Latino soul/rock band. It was the first time since I was a child at the Ward Theatre in Kingston, watching the Pantomime "Busha Bluebeard," that I found myself in a sea of Black people in a theatre. I had a special kind of feeling I cannot describe.

On my return from holiday, I reported to my new Station, RAF Abingdon, where I had done my high jump training five years earlier. I no longer took part in my usual sports. Instead, I decided to work out in the gym. First, I was persuaded to compete in the RAF Championship in the 400 metres (as the distance was now run in the RAF), so I put in some training sessions on the track. I finished in the middle of the pack. They'd also heard that I'd boxed in Cyprus and assumed I was a proper boxer, despite my explanation. I surprised myself by agreeing to become a sparring partner with the boxing team. I thought it would be harmless with the protective gear. It wasn't too long before I broke my thumb in one of the sparring sessions.

My role at Abingdon included crane operating, sometimes fitting propellers onto planes. There are two ways to lower a weight being held on a crane. One is to lower the jib (near-horizontal beam that carries the hook and cable). The other is to reel out the cable carrying the hook and the load, which in this case, was the propellor. It's difficult to line up the hole at the centre of a propellor with the shaft on the plane. After taking hand signals from the staff on the ground for ages – up, down, up, down – I did the unthinkable. I jumped out of the cab to inspect how the centre of the propellor and the shaft lined up, ignoring the instructions to just carry out the instructions as given, as was the custom. I realised that lowering the propellor by the jib would be better because of the noticeably short distance needed to line up the hole and the shaft. I climbed back into the crane cab and did just that. It worked. The junior airmen clapped. The senior ones were stony-faced.

One day, I responded to a circular seeking skiers to go to Scotland for a week. All we needed was to take our annual leave for the week. I was surprised to find that I had been accepted as one of the coach drivers. When I explained that I had applied as a skier, they were surprised and asked about my skiing experience. I told them about my Cyprus skiing experience and pointed out that Aviemore to which the trip was headed, was supposed to be ideal for new skiers – according to the notice that had been circulated. I was later told that all the places had been taken and if anyone dropped out, I'd be the No.1 replacement. I withdrew my name from the list.

I also took new drivers out for further training around the Oxford area. There was one young man who seemed to have trouble gauging distances and tended to pull out dangerously in front of traffic. I insisted he should have an eye test. It turned out he was blind in his right eye. When asked how he got away with it at the driving school and at other medicals, he said whenever he was asked to look with his other eye, he simply switched the hand with which he covered his right eye.

A couple of months later, I was told to report to the RAF Careers Information Service (CIO), Kingsway, London. On arrival, I met two other Corporal drivers, both white. We were told that the CIO was looking for a replacement driver for the Nottingham office. We were called in one by one for an interview then asked to wait. The first driver called in after the interviews, returned with his envelope and told the other one that he was returning to camp. He then congratulated him on his new job. The second driver avoided eye contact with me when he returned, grabbed his hat and belongings, and left. I was finally called in and congratulated on being successful. I was being posted to the CIO, Nottingham. Being single, I'd live on camp at RAF Newton on the east side of Nottingham and drive the Land Rover to the office each day.

I was now assigned to the RAF Recruitment Office, and spent a few weeks there before going on the RAF External Recruitment Course. That course lay the foundation for so many of the things I've achieved in my life. I'm so grateful for the opportunity to have done it. The attendees were both non-commissioned and commissioned officers and we all did the same basic course, except for special management stuff for the Commissioned Officers. I knew I had to perform well. Whereas I had passed all my RAF courses, my Record of Service Booklet shows this recruitment course as the only one for which I had received a "credit." I believe my early years of elocution contests prepared me for it, as other more-senior course members had trouble with the public speaking and interview practice elements.

I was put on reception duties at the Recruitment Office, greeting casual visitors and giving out information about careers in the Air Force. I also drove the mobile office – an articulated vehicle. When the back doors opened, the huge interior space revealed an office with advertising displays and booklets about trades in the RAF. I drove it mainly to shows at faraway places where you didn't have an RAF base nearby. These included the Carlisle Agricultural Show, a Gymkhana at Speke Airport (now the John Lennon), and Dalbeattie in Scotland. We also visited market towns and places where factories had closed, and people were out of work. Later, the mobile unit expanded to include a caravan, which I towed with the Land Rover. The interior was also like an office with displays. We used it for smaller venues and shorter runs from which we'd return at the end of the day – like the Spondon Carnival, (just outside Nottingham), and nearby Derbyshire and Nottinghamshire towns.

There are four incidents I'd like to share. First, when at the Carlisle Agricultural Show, I tried to position the truck trailer office by reversing from behind the main area, so that the back of the vehicle was by the main thoroughfare. The Flight Lieutenant insisted on directing me. He was clearly unaware that in reversing an articulated vehicle, one turns the steering in the opposite direction to manoeuvre the trailer. When I attempted to get out of the cab and look for myself, he ordered me back in and continued directing me. Fed up, I jumped out the cab and went over to one of the Sergeants and spoke softly to him, explaining why I needed to carry out the manoeuvre on my own. He understood and went to speak with the Flight Lieutenant who then walked away. As if by magic, I positioned the vehicle perfectly first time, on my own. There was an element of luck in it, but they weren't to know that.

The second incident was my performance review meeting with Squadron Leader Jarvis. At the end of it, he turned his writing pad so I could read the last uncovered sentence, excused himself and left the room. The sentence read: "Corporal Panton must be employed on the full range of recruiting duties for which he is employed." Up to then, I was only doing reception duties. Never full recruitment interviews. I learnt that the previous driver never did full interviews. Apparently, my senior colleagues didn't like the idea of a driver doing the same job as them. It shouldn't have been so, because we, the NCOs, made recommendations only, supported by the notes of our interviews. The commissioned officer conducted a second interview and reached his own decision. From then on, I was assigned to the interviewing team.

The third incident is this: I noticed that my colleagues had a habit of making up their minds about potential recruits before the official interviews. They did this much more with the women. It was as if they were judging a beauty contest. They took it up on themselves to comment aloud on those whom I interviewed, I believe, to influence my decision. One day, I interviewed two young men who were friends and didn't recommend them for service. My colleagues were aghast. They made it plain they disagreed with me and I suspect they said something to Squadron Leader Jarvis who, I'm sure, reached his own independent decision to offer them a place in the RAF. A few months later, one of the young men visited the office to chat with one of my colleagues. They'd apparently kept in touch. Both had been discharged from the service on medical grounds. I didn't know the details. The point is, two training places were wasted.

The fourth and final incident occurred when an angry father burst into the office to talk to the officer who had dared to reject his daughter for service. I stood up, as was the custom, and was towering over him. He looked me up and down. I was in peak fitness then."She didn't tell me you were coloured. Shite…never mind." He turned and walked out. I don't know if he'd known I was Black he wouldn't have bothered, not wanting to appear prejudiced; or if he just didn't want to take on a big Black fellow. I never said anything to anyone about it, but I was sure I was not the one who had interviewed his daughter.

It was a lonely time for me at the office. Whenever I wasn't interviewing, I was manning Reception which was a room in the front of the office. I was the only single person in the office and wasn't a drinker or smoker, and hated pubs. I was determined not to get married before reaching at least my mid-thirties, fearing loss of my freedom to do whatever I wanted – at will and at short notice. I accepted my loneliness and it helped me to decide to not continue beyond the nine years to which I was committed. This was even after Squadron Leader Jarvis tried to get me to sit for the Sergeants' Exam. He felt that after the Recruiting Office, it would be up, up, up for me. I knew I couldn't carry on as a driver and even if I got to the top rank of Warrant Officer, I wouldn't be satisfied with the lack of intellectual challenge, irrespective of rank. To be honest, I didn't think about taking up such challenges outside the RAF in my own time. I began to understand what the recruiting officer meant when he told me to consider clerical work, instead of being a driver. I considered switching trades and, after making enquiries, I was invited to RAF St. Athan for a chat about becoming a physical education instructor. I soon changed my mind and cancelled the appointment. I decided I wouldn't do my Class 2 Exam (necessary for promotion consideration), afraid that if I harboured the idea of promotion, I would stay in the service. I was going to leave in July 1973 at the end of my nine-year service.

I soon learnt that the practice of dismissing someone from their job because they applied to join the RAF was not uncommon. I think updated employment law gives some protection to employees today.

My social life improved when I met and made friends with a young Nottingham couple, Maurice, and Grace Henry, and got to know their family and friends. I no longer needed to dash down to London as frequently as before on weekends. I eventually became godfather to their daughter Marsha. We are still friends to this day, nearly 50 years later.

At Abingdon, I'd already started to prepare for life after the RAF. I had enquired about attending the Abingdon Adult Education college, but the subjects offered, and the times of attendance made it impossible. I was, however, pursuing correspondence courses in journalism, export marketing and Spanish. My office colleagues thought I was nuts when, in October 1972, I accumulated my leave and spent a month at a private school in Barcelona.

There were only six students in the class: four women and two men. There was a 30-ish Californian who wouldn't say what she did; a French au pair; a Swiss farmer; a Filipino secretary; and a Scottish student; and me. The local people spoke Catalan amongst themselves but accommodated us by speaking Spanish in our presence. They even told us where to get proper locally flavoured dishes. "Watch where the old fellows go, and being a student of the language, you'd be welcomed," they told us.

For the first week, as a group, we went for walks in along Las Ramblas, a major boulevard, and to a bull fight, the Barcelona Football Club Stadium, cafes, bars, and other places of interest. We each also explored on our own. I met an American young lady who was travelling Europe and we went to a nightclub called Dos Mil Uno (2001, twenty nine years in the future), a few times. It's sometimes hard to believe that we are now 20 years past 2001.

The US Aircraft Carrier Roosevelt was on a goodwill trip to Barcelona and as I had my RAF Identity Card with me, I was able to go aboard and was shown around. I'll never forget the awe I felt when transferring from the motorboat to the carrier that was a little offshore. The massive piece of steel didn't seem to have any right being afloat. Once on board, I was shown around. The hangars with the planes and cranes and other support machinery made me wonder even more about the engineering of the vessel.

We found out that October 14th, a Saturday, was the date commemorating when Columbus set sail for the "New World." It was, therefore, a holiday weekend. I and my Californian, Swiss and Filipino colleagues, decided to spend the weekend on a visit to the village of Cadaques where the painter Salvador Dali lived. The seaside resort was deserted, as it was the end of the holiday season. We found a very hospitable restaurant and spent hours there, lingering over a late breakfast then also having lunch. We only had to pay for lunch. The rest was on the house. They told us that being students of the language, we could visit Dali's home and gave us directions. It was a white painted cottage. The resident housekeeper, looking like a nurse in her all-white outfit, showed us around a room that was basically an art gallery. Dali wasn't there. Just being there was exciting for the Swiss who knew a lot about Dali. I first heard about Dali at the school so, for me, it was a case that I could say, I'd visited Dali's house.

Near the end of the course, the Californian had a visit from a friend at a café who began her conversation with the statement that the Captain wanted to know how she was getting on. She was immediately stopped from saying anymore. We thought then that they were probably police officers. The Swiss guy and Perla, the Filipino, became a couple and were seriously considering marriage.

RAF Newton where I lived, was an aircraft electronics training school that included foreign military personnel from Nigeria, Malaysia, Jordan, and Iran. I was friendly with the guys from all these places. In summer 1972, I ran my last 400- metre race, winning the Station competition. To put in my study hours, I was in bed at around 8 p.m. because the noise of the drinkers quieted down by midnight. That's when I got up and did my correspondence studies till 3 or 4 a.m., then back to bed for two to three hours. It worked well for me.

In preparation for civilian life, the RAF provide courses on jobhunting. Many of the older folks who had served many years and had a trade or skill they'd be continuing, sometimes did DIY courses like bricklaying, plumbing and joinery. Most of the training were carried out in the government's training centres. When I was summoned to see the Education Officer at RAF Newton, I did my research and found I could do just about anything I wanted to within certain cost and time limits and a one-month French course was possible. I contacted a few French language schools in London to enquire about a one-month intensive French course. None was available. I settled on a full-time, three-week, intensive course at Mentor for Languages in Central London. When I told the Education Officer what I'd chosen, he didn't seem to want to believe his ears. He was even more surprised when I was able to hand over the details I'd received from Mentor for Languages. He was eventually supportive and asked how I planned to use my French. I told him that with a second foreign language I stood a better chance of getting an export job. On hearing that I'd already started studying French by Linguaphone in preparation, he seemed pleased. I received authorization to do the course.

At Mentor for Languages, we were a class of about ten. The others were mainly secretaries and young executives of companies, plus two Asian sisters from Uganda. Except for the Ugandans, our studies were being paid for by our employers. The teachers, all French natives, told me that my attendance was monitored by visiting "officials" three times, the most they'd ever experienced for any of their students. They thought it was funny. One day, one of the Ugandan sisters asked me about arranged marriages within my community. When I explained it was not done on a formal basis (although families, of course, introduced nice boys to nice girls), she burst into tears. She was being forced into an arranged marriage. She wept several days in class. Everybody soon knew why.

The French course was better than I'd hoped, and I did very well. The teachers hardly ever spoke English in class, and they put my achievement down to having studied Spanish and Latin. A few years later, my wife and I visited some friends in Geneva, Switzerland. On the way back, my wife noticed we were given the wrong boarding passes. Our luggage was already on a plane bound for Prague, Czechoslovakia. We went back to the booking clerk who refused to send someone to get our luggage off the plane. I got angry and spoke louder than normal in the hope that someone would try and help us. It worked. When we walked away from the desk, my wife pointed out to me that I had spoken in French the entire time. I suspect though, that I must have thrown in a considerable number of English words.

On my last day in the office, my colleagues gathered round and had a little drink with me and wished me well. They made me a present of an engraved map of Nottingham and a two pound premium bond. The Warrant Officer still thought I was making a mistake leaving the RAF. He figured that if I did just 13 more years, with periodic promotions, I'd retire with a decent pension at age 43. I thought he was the sort of person who'd make sure I was sent to Northern Ireland where the most danger lay then. Also, what he didn't realise was that when I was in Cyprus, I had seen how the wives and children of the commissioned officers and senior NCOs pushed their weight around in social circumstances or say, the clinic, wielding their husband's ranks. I'd already decided that I'd never expose my wife and family to such carryings-on, which couldn't always be avoided.

My last day of RAF service would be 5 July 1973. I was progressing well with my journalism course but was a bit casual with the export marketing as I already knew a bit about it and was familiar with a lot of the terminology. Therefore, one day, I received my corrected marketing lesson with lots of writing in red ink. I decided to put a bit more effort into it. One of the exercises for the journalism course was a repeat of something I'd done before – writing an article for local and national readership. This time it was an exercise whereby I was called out to a fire involving commercial property at about 3 a.m. I would be tested on the details I included or excluded for the different readerships. Strangely, what hit me halfway through the exercise was the realisation that I had been looking to do a job that could involve me getting out of my bed at all hours of the night when I might be the father of young children. I'd already worked 24-7 at RAF Abingdon. I'd been called out of bed to take a crane to help the fire service rescue a lorry driver who was stuck in his cab after crashing his lorry into a house in the nearby village of Wantage. No, I thought. I'm getting older and don't fancy jumping out of my bed in the middle of the night to write a report on anything. Despite having completed numerous exercises including visiting a magistrates' court and writing a report on a case, I decided to turn my back on journalism. I decided to strengthen my hand for export marketing by taking on another correspondence course: commerce.

CHAPTER SIX
Back to Civilian life

On leaving the RAF, I went to Paris for a weekend with a girlfriend. We met with an elderly friend of hers who briefed us on using the Metro and advised us on the best places to visit and when. It was a lovely, hot summer weekend and I had an opportunity to practice my French. We stayed at a hotel run by an Algerian family on the Place de la Concorde, and took in the usual tourist attractions, including the Cathedral Notre-Dame.

Back in London, Dad, at 62, wasn't coping well with the cold and had been in hospital with bronchial asthma. The tropics was calling him home. He decided to take early retirement and leave. Mother Dear was resigned to returning as well, provided Dad returned first and built the house – just a couple of bedrooms with the essentials. She had to be comfortable on arrival. Dad understood. I went to see him off at Southampton.

I was 30 years old and still not settled. My parents weren't bothered. Well, that's what they said. They said they had confidence in me. They felt I'd be alright. I turned to my study plans. I applied for a degree course in Latin American studies at Portsmouth Polytechnic. It was open to adults who didn't have the normal 'A' level entry requirements but had a reasonable knowledge of Spanish and could convince the Poly that they had the intellectual ability to complete the course. I checked with the education authorities and they confirmed I would qualify for a grant if accepted. After my interview with Dr. Martin at the Poly, he told me he would accept me but had reservations about the extensive travelling I had done, in the RAF, Spain and the USA. He preferred that I display a certain stability which would indicate that I would return to the Poly after my study year abroad in Venezuela or Mexico, adding that they had a high dropout rate after the year abroad. He invited me to apply for the term starting September 1974, the following year, adding that he guaranteed that if I continued with my correspondence studies, he'd accept me then. Given that I really wanted to do a Spanish studies course, I decided to go to Spain instead. Thoughts of the USA also resurfaced. I thought their system of "course credits" would suit me fine.

I decided to get casual jobs for a few weeks, while I continued my correspondence studies and figured out my next move. I decided on night jobs so that I could spend time in the libraries during the day, and save more. My night jobs included packing biscuits at a Peak Freans biscuit factory, and stacking crates of soft drink at a Canada Dry warehouse. Most of the night workers were students from Africa, India, and the Caribbean. Some openly took pills to keep themselves awake. I found the work exhausting, so I decided to try something else. I had a Ford Zodiac car and thought about working as a minicab driver, but the car was too old for that. I decided I'd go to Spain. There had to be a suitable course of study.

In preparation for Spain, I found a night-time chauffeuring job which ensured that I worked at the weekends when I'd earn more tips and couldn't go clubbing and so would save more. Norwood Motors, situated at the entrance of Tulse Hill Railway station in South London, welcomed me with open arms, and I found rented accommodation nearby.

Norwood Motors clients with the Company included Harry Carpenter (a TV boxing commentator); Sam Silkin, later to become attorney general in Harold Wilson's government; the Morleys (Julia of the Miss World pageant and her husband Eric); a host of Philips, Shell and Unilever executives who lived in posh houses in nearby Dulwich Village, some owned by their companies; and Ministry of Defence (MOD) staffers. I found out later that my employer was pleased to have me drive their MOD clients whenever I was on duty. My shift was even switched to days, at times, including during the Farnborough Air Show, so I would be the one to drive MOD personnel. I'd like to mention three chauffeuring incidents that have stuck with me.

The first has to do with commentator Harry Carpenter. On the way from the airport, upon his return from the Commonwealth Games in New Zealand, he was eager to tell me that he'd be going down to Jamaica for the Frazier-Foreman fight. I took the opportunity to show off my boxing knowledge, having been a great fan of the BBC's long-time programme, America's Fight of the Week, on their Saturday Grandstand. He was impressed when I talked about Muhammad Ali's early fights with Alejandro Lavorante, Archie Moore, Doug Jones, and Alex Miteff, among others. I also mentioned boxers of other weights who were popular at the same time, like Skeeter McClure. Harry said, because of the conversation, it was the quickest ride home he'd had. He gave me a huge tip. It was a practical lesson that having a wide knowledge and being able to have a decent conversation, initiated by the client, of course, could bring hidden benefits.

The second incident occurred when driving a senior army officer to a boxing tournament in Windsor. He engaged me in chit-chat and, after a little while, asked which regiment I served in. When I told him, I was never in the army, he said: "The RAF then." I laughed.

"Why did you say that Sir?" I asked.

"The way you wear your chauffeur's cap. It's a perfect fit and it sits level on your head. You were taught to do that in the military. Also, the way you say "sir," not forced, not cumbersome, not emphasized. Kinda natural like."

"Well, you certainly have me there sir. RAF," I replied. He continued talking about all sorts of things and was becoming more and more relaxed. He said he didn't really want to be going to the boxing match, but he had to fulfil his duties. His accent, which started as a typical upper-class, began to lose its shine and he started to use Scottish words like "laddie" and "wee" (small). When there was a break in his monologue, I asked where in Scotland he was from. (With my nine years in the RAF and having visited Scotland, I could spot it.) He let out a belly-laugh and said, "I guess the wee dram o' whiskey is kicking in," and he laughed even more. He never said where he was from and I never asked again. He also gave me a big tip. That incident made me realise just how much I had become a 'military person' without knowing it, and that even after nearly a year out of uniform, it was still a part of me.

The third story is about driving a couple of Japanese businessmen from the Heathrow airport to their hotel in Central London. I'd made it my duty to read foreign business news to help my correspondence studies. By chance, I'd been following developments in Japan. After World War 2, the Americans imposed restrictions on the Japanese that forbade them from manufacturing aircraft. The ban was later lifted, and the Japanese built a twin-engine, turboprop passenger plane, the NAMC YS-11, but were ceasing production in 1974. They were also compulsorily purchasing land to build a massive new airport in Narita, just outside Tokyo, and facing a multitude of problems with the local people and trades unions who opposed the building of the airport and there were clashes with the police. Now, Japanese clients were not usually that talkative to me, their chauffeur. So, it was a surprise when these two gentlemen wanted to know where I was from and so on. After answering their questions, I jumped in with a question of my own about their aircraft, making sure I called it by its proper name. They became excited that I knew about it and talked eagerly, dropping in some Japanese words when their excitement affected their English vocabulary. Grabbing the opportunity when they took a breather, I asked them about the Narita airport and how things were going. Again, they became excited and willingly updated me. Finally, one of them asked me what my regular job was and didn't want to believe me when I told him that being a chauffeur was the only job I had. I was then forced to tell him about my studies and plans to study further in Spain. Again, I got a huge tip.

By Easter 1974, Dad had returned from Jamaica and he, Mother Dear and my little brother Ludovic left to live in the house he'd built there. I started to look for a suitable course at a Spanish university. I concentrated on the south, having already been to Barcelona in the northeast, I wanted warm weather. Granada and Malaga became my choices. I found a one-year diploma course at Malaga University. The subjects were language, literature, art, geography, and history, all taught in Spanish. In addition, I could attend any lectures in the main university, if there was space for me, and I if didn't interrupt by asking the lecturers or students any questions. The course would run from July to the following May. I calculated I'd be able to afford it. Two weeks before the course was due to start, I gave a week's notice at work. They were not at all pleased. They paid me a week in advance and said I didn't have to work the notice period. It was difficult to tell whether they genuinely wished we well as they said they did.

While at RAF Cardington in 1965, I became pen-friends with a Mexican girl, Gloria. We continued corresponding all the years to Cyprus and back. In 1973, she came to London with a friend to improve her English. She had everything arranged, including a part-time hotel cleaning job. We met in Earls Court where she shared accommodation with other girls. It was an exciting meeting for both of us. We were both surprised that we spoke each other's language sufficiently well for us not to need any help. The only thing that was a bit difficult for me, was getting used to a blonde. All the photos she had sent me were with her natural dark hair. One day when we were alone and she was in the kitchen, I began reciting her university graduation speech. She turned around, smiling. Then when she realized I wasn't reading it (she had sent me a copy), she was open-mouthed and stuck for words. I'd used it to improve my Spanish vocabulary, then decided to learn it and say it out loud. She started to cry. (I don't know why women like to cry so much.)

When she met my folks, she and Mother Dear chatted in Spanish. Mother Dear had been away from Spanish-speaking Costa Rica for 45 years, and she spoke in halting sentences to start with, but eventually was able to converse reasonably well. She was so surprised at herself that she dabbed her tears. She thought she'd lost it all. I regretted not pushing her a bit more when she declined to answer me in Spanish at times. Gloria returned to Mexico in 1974, shortly before I left for Spain, and she and Mother Dear corresponded for some years afterwards. After some time, Mother Dear told me she got married.

CHAPTER SEVEN
Spain, Malaga University

I found that a cheap way to get to Malaga would be by train to Dover: the ferry to Calais, and a train from Calais to Malaga, changing trains in Paris. Decision made. It was an uneventful journey to Paris where we had a long stop-over. As it was getting dark, I phoned a dentist from Martinique who was a friend of the elderly lady I'd met on my previous visit to Paris. He invited me to pop by for an hour or so, as he wasn't far from the train station. Soon I was back in French mode, instead of Spanish, because although he spoke English, his French wife didn't. I was so, so glad I had done the course at Mentor for Languages. Both thought I should have been married by then and were sure I'd be married to a Spaniard before the year was out. I was 31 years old. They made me a meal and gave me sandwiches to take with me before we bid each other farewell.

The journey from Paris to the French-Spanish border seemed to take ages. There were many young people with rucksacks, and they all looked tired. Everybody slept. At the border, there was a lot of clunking as our train pitched forwards and backwards as carriages were removed or added. It was nearly an hour before we were on our way again. By daybreak, we were travelling through lush, green, breath-taking hills and valleys. Places didn't seem to matter as there wasn't much to see from the lonely railway tracks that seemed to be pushed into the wilds away from villages and towns. Then, almost without warning, we were moving through a red-dirt plateau that reminded me of some of the cowboy films I'd seen. There'd been a change of passengers in my carriage along the way.

The first being at the border. Still, there wasn't much conversation. I don't know if the noise of the wheels on the tracks anything had to do with it. Then we came to halt in the middle of nowhere. It began to get hot. There was no more passing breeze created by the moving train to cool us down. Apart from people opening their doors and fanning themselves, there was no fussing. It seemed as if it was an everyday occurrence for the regular travellers, or just what was to be expected by the others, especially by the non-Spaniards. After nearly an hour, we were on our way again. There was no explanation from the train crew. At least not in the third class carriage I was in. We arrived in Malaga in the afternoon.

I had a few days before enrolment, so I decided to visit Marbella where the rich at that time hung out. I jumped on a bus and booked into Pension Mama Louisa, a cheap hostel in a narrow back street. There was little privacy. The other occupants were three young Scandinavian men, two Dutch young ladies and Anthony, a lean, super-fit American, the only one of us with his own room. I thought he was a bit crazy. He latched on to me to tell me tales of the extra-terrestrial people with whom he was in contact. He was, however, a very pleasant fellow, always smiling. He took me to the cheap eating places and told me to search them out in Malaga. Anthony said he'd been in Marbella for nearly a year but didn't feel the need to learn Spanish because his gesticulations made up for the English words the Spaniards didn't know. I spent two nights there before heading back to Malaga and checking out the list of places to stay provided by the university. Some were with families and others were in hostels.

After visiting two families in Malaga, I settled on the first hostel I went to – Hostal San Lorenzo in Calle Pinzon. It was a modern brick building, just around the corner from the British Embassy's Malaga office. It was close to the waterfront, banks, shops, and restaurants. The top floor was occupied by the caretaker and his family. The hostel catered for about 20 people, who were a mix of short-term visitors and longer-term "residents." Breakfast and an evening meal were provided. I had a small room that overlooked a road, and my own bathroom. A tiny balcony was shared with the room next door and separated by a low wall. I calculated that I could manage to stay there for about nine months without any real problem. I opened a local bank account and transferred three months' money from my UK account. All the occupants at the time were working Spaniards from out of town. There was a pharmacist, a policewoman, a bank clerk, and others. My balcony neighbour was a man who had a fighting Cockerel. Don't know where he kept it normally, but on fighting evenings, he'd talk to it in loving terms and stroked its head and feathers down its neck and back. It was such a gentle bird. Difficult to imagine it being the sort of fighter I'd seen in films.

The hostel was owned by a former Malaga football player and his wife. He bought boatloads of fish from the local fishermen then sold them in smaller quantities to retailers and restaurants. His wife and her four sisters and a brother ran the hostel. One of the sisters was a nurse, one a student at the university, and the other two split their time between looking after their mother and the hostel. I was soon treated like a member of the family, and my Spanish improved quickly, as none of them was interested in speaking English.

Malaga is in the Andalusian region and is both the name of the province and the capital city. It has a large port that was being modernized while I was there. Many new buildings were going up: houses and commercial buildings, including hotels. The restrictions put in place by General Franco were loosening as the end of his dictatorship rule was approaching. Students buoyed by the civil rights and anti-Vietnam demonstrations in the US felt more comfortable in demonstrating. Unfortunately for them, the Guardia Civil were no less fierce in keeping them in check.

My classmates were from Australia, Belgium, England, France, Germany, Sweden, Switzerland, and the US. All the young ladies, except for my friends English Jenny and Aussie Hazel, lived with families. Hazel said she just wanted to do something different after divorcing her navy husband. Tubiorne, from Sweden, who also lived in a privately rented accommodation, said he was preparing to become an air steward. We were quite a friendly bunch. We had our lessons in the city centre, close to where I was staying. I spoke better Spanish than most. With the other subjects, I thought I'd read enough, but I soon found that I had quite a lot of catching up to do in literature and art. A memorable incident for me was my first day in a mainstream geography lesson. The lecturer started talking from the moment he entered the classroom, and it took me about a minute to realise that the lecture was underway from the moment he entered the room, making his way to the front of the class. I didn't have too much difficulty understanding him, but I couldn't take notes properly. When reflecting on what happened, I realized I had a real problem. I didn't know how to take notes – what to include and what to exclude. I'd been studying for years by correspondence and had grown accustomed to reading passages, then going over them again, highlighting or underling key sentences. Taking appropriate notes was a skill I knew I had to master and would be essential for the mainstream classes I would be attending. I wondered how I might have fared had I gone to Portsmouth Polytechnic.

In attending the geography and history lessons at the main university, I realized how similar life in rural Spain had been to that in the villages in Jamaica when the immigration to England was in full flow. In the 1950s and 60s, the economy of Spain's south coast was taking off with a hotel and housing boom. It was also the peak of immigration of Spanish men to work in the car factories in Germany and other European countries. Many Spanish villages were bereft of their able-bodied men as they moved away from subsistence farming to construction and factory work. Families were torn apart as the men forged new relationships wherever they went. And, as the progressive young women decided to head to the south coast as well, the villages consisted mainly of old men, old women, and children. In Jamaica, women suffered additional trauma when many who were expecting to join their menfolk would be in turmoil as the men sent for someone else; often for someone much younger. It was a little distressing as I reflected on Jamaica's experience.

A Cuban sugar transporter was the first Cuban ship to visit the Port of Malaga since Castro's revolution. By chance (or perhaps it trailed it there), a US naval vessel was berthed nearby. I went to the port and after a chat with the guard, and the ship's medic came to see me. He examined my passport and accepting that I was, indeed, a UK student and from his neighbouring island of Jamaica, he allowed me to come aboard. Looking across at the Americans, I imagined that they didn't seem too pleased with the presence of the Cuban ship. I visited the ship a few times for the few days it was in port, and the ship's doctor and another crew member visited me at the hostel where they had a good chat with the folks there.

I soon realized how poor I was in comparison to my colleagues when on some Monday mornings they talked about the places they had visited over the weekend – some of the places featured in the geography, history, literature, and art lessons. Being in the Andalusian region, a lot of the lectures centred on Andalusia. I decided I had to go on a couple of visits, and I joined three others on a bus trip to Granada. It was uphill most of the way – winding roads and beautiful scenery of the mountainside and the sea. Sometimes huge rocks just sat on a piece of land making you wonder how they got there. The terrain reminded me of my journey from Lancashire to South Wales when I was in the RAF. We walked along on cobblestones to the top of the hill to the Alhambra, the main reason for visiting Granada. There was an immediate sense of mystery. A fortress built by the Moors, the Alhambra overlooks the Granada Plains, and is one of the most famous buildings in Spain. For the Andalusians, it is the most important. In ancient times, it had three sections: The Alcazaba, the military base that housed guards and their families; an area that had the palaces for the Sultan and his entourage; and the Medina where court officials lived and worked. Visitors treated the place with reverence, being as silent as in a library. I felt I was back in time. (Future generations might draw a parallel with Gibraltar being the domain of a foreign country for so long.) The Alhambra also has a link with the western discoveries attributed to Christopher Columbus because it was after King Ferdinand and Queen Isabella conquered Granada following centuries of Islamic rule that they agreed to fund Columbus's journey. One of the surprises of the visit was the eeriness of midday on a Sunday with most bars and restaurants closed. We soon found that the top football club, Real Madrid, was playing Granada – in Granada – to a full stadium.

My next visit was to Cordoba with my Swiss classmate. We left the Friday evening and returned Sunday. Again, the province and its capital carry the same name. Cordoba was quite a contrast to Granada. It's flat, lying to the northwest of Granada in a valley through which runs the Guadalquivir River at the south of the Morena Mountains. It's also an extremely hot place, reaching temperatures of up to 40C/104F in the summer. It was conquered by the Romans before the arrival of the Moors and has a Jewish quarter. The star attraction of Cordoba is a fantastic mosque with curved arches that give the appearance of a tunnel when viewed from a distance.–The mosque was turned into a church by the Catholic Spaniards after they re-took Cordoba from the Moors, even though they didn't ruin its unique architecture. Cordoba was so important to the Spanish monarch that Queen Isabella insisted Columbus set sail from there to the Western World. The city had many interesting Moorish attractions, including geometric gardens that reflect Muslim conventions of science, geometry, and order. Balconies with hanging baskets of flowers adorned the narrow streets, as groups of citizens of all ages danced together happily in the squares on the Saturday afternoon. They seemed to be dancing for themselves, as they ignored the tourists who took their pictures.

I had wondered why even the small-looking restaurants in Barcelona, Malaga and elsewhere, had such large seating areas. I learnt that because of the civil war (July 1936 to April 1939), where fathers, sons and brothers were on different sides of the political arena and therefore took up arms against each other. The mistrust among family members was so strong, that a neutral meeting place was necessary for family gatherings. The restaurant was that place. The system of restaurant gatherings has continued to this day and it seems that many of the younger generation didn't know how the custom developed.

I visited other towns and villages close to Malaga and learnt why seeing them in their true form was so important to their presence in the lectures. The trips ruined my budget, so I had to find some extra money. I decided to teach English privately. Despite my years in England and my years in the RAF I never quite took on the full English accent. It was a handicap to my getting students. I decided to mimic the way my French teachers taught, eliminating the student's own language during the lesson. I was lucky that word got around that my teaching method, including grammar, mirrored their books. Maribin, the daughter of the caretaker of the building, was my first student. We met on their balcony, her mother always close by, and our conversations included things we could see mountain, cloud, sky, sea, building, car, seaport, ships, beach, tree, building, road, shops, people. It was a panoramic view, so there was an endless choice. We then dealt with things inside the home. I got her to associate the items with the English words instead of doing a translation in her head. It worked. I soon found that her mother, who never once said a word of interruption, was an excellent student herself. We laughed about it but what could I do? I couldn't ask her to pay for lessons too.

My social life was varied. Unlike what my Parisian friends had predicted, I didn't marry a Spaniard. Didn't even come close. I did have a few Spanish female friends but not serious enough for any such thoughts. I found myself going to bars from time to time with other students with whom I became friendly. The bars sold a lot of wine and the smell was more pleasant than in the UK. My friends were typically between 18 and 22, a few years younger than me. The young men, for whom a short military service was compulsory, couldn't understand why someone would serve nine years in the military on a voluntary basis. They thought me odd. I went to night-time beach parties. A non-invited guest (or two) was always on the fringes. My friends explained that the folks were police informers whose role was to report if they engaged in any political discussions, something that was prohibited in Franco's Spain. When I was planning my return to the UK, I asked myself the question: Where was I going to stay? I contacted a cousin who I used to visit a lot in London when I returned from Cyprus. She said it would be fine to stay with her and her family until I sorted myself out. The cheapest way back was by coach. It would be a long journey home.

The bus started its journey in Marbella on the Wednesday afternoon. I boarded the bus in Malaga, and we left the coast road and headed for Granada where we picked up more passengers before re-joining the coast road towards Barcelona. We made a couple of stops at holiday resorts on the way until the coach had a full load. We arrived in Barcelona just before dusk on the Thursday evening and headed to our hotel for the overnight stop. We were several to a room. We left Barcelona on the Friday morning and travelled all day and night with a few motorway stops, passing the outskirts of Paris on the Saturday morning on the way to the Calais Ferry. We arrived at Victoria Station in the early afternoon. As you might guess, it was before the wonderful motorways that are now prevalent in Spain and France. I was tired. Tired as if I'd been doing the driving.

CHAPTER EIGHT
Civil Service, Early Years

_____

As planned, I lived with my cousin in north London for a while after my return, before finding my own rental accommodation. The government employment office in Wood Green sent me to an export marketing job in Soho with a company that had links with a few Spanish-speaking South American countries. I was introduced to the staff in the department I would be working in and told that I'd receive a letter from them in a couple of days. On not hearing from them, I phoned but was never able to speak to anyone in authority. I went back to see the officers in the employment office. They told me they'd been advised by the company to remove the vacancy because I got the job. Confused, they phoned the company. After coming off the phone, the gentleman went into the offices at the back. Another person came out and told me he was sorry, but it seems there was a mix-up but not to worry, because the manager at the employment office wanted to see me the following morning. When I returned next day, I was introduced to the manager, Harry Friar – former Flight Lieutenant Harry Friar, who'd also previously worked in an RAF Recruiting Office.

"I've been through your notes and although the interviews we conduct here aren't as in-depth as in the RAF, I could use you for a while. I could take you on as a temp. You will be best placed to see the jobs as they come in. We won't stand in your way of getting what you want. What do you say?" It was matter-of-fact. Straight to the point. I thought that if he, a former RAF Flight Lieutenant could be working there, why shouldn't I? I didn't hesitate in saying yes. Then he explained that he only had power for local recruitment at clerical assistant level (the lowest grade). He waited for a reaction. I said that would be fine. How could I say otherwise? Then he went on to say that once I was taken on, he could promote me in the afternoon to clerical officer, also on a temporary basis. It was my introduction to the quirks in the employment rules agreed between the civil service and the unions when it comes to local recruitment.

I turned up as planned on the Monday morning and completed the necessary paperwork. I was at 32, a temporary clerical assistant in the civil service. I was shown around the offices and introduced to members of staff. After lunch, I was invited to sit in the first aid room, given a sheet of paper and a pen and asked to write a description of the room. I couldn't believe it. I wrote it, including its importance to health and safety, easy access, wide door for a hospital trolley and wheelchair. I was enjoying myself. After I handed it in, Mr. Friar came to me, shook my hand, and said, "Right, you're now a temporary clerical officer. We have work to do." He told me that was it for the day and he'd see me the next day. I was placed to shadow the disablement resettlement officer who was a cigar smoker. I couldn't share a room space with her. One or two of the staff weren't too pleased when they found that I'd soon be interviewing jobseekers. It didn't matter. I quickly learnt the forms I had to use and the essential details I had to elicit from the jobseekers. At that time, many Ugandan Asians were fleeing Idi Amin's regime. Some of them objected to being interviewed by me, a Black man. Some aborted their visit and returned when they hoped a white colleague would interview them. The younger ones who I saw were generally in their mid-thirties and mostly well educated. Many of the young men were accountants. They had a tough time getting jobs. Often their failure was because they were more qualified than their immediate bosses who feared losing their position or having the Ugandan Asians as equals after a short time. In December 1975, a few months after I started, I transferred my temporary status to become a permanent civil servant at clerical officer level. After a while, I was sent on an induction course.

In September 1976, I received a telephone call from someone identifying himself as Jerry Brown, the area personnel manager. I realised he thought I should have known who he was. He invited me to come the following day to meet him at Selkirk House, in High Holborn, London. Again, he seemed to think I should know where it was. Then he told me why. He had taken on the new job of being the London regional manager of a new government project and in putting his start-up staff together, he wanted me as part of his team. He remembered me from the induction course. Yes, he was a former major in the British Indian Army who delighted in speaking in one of the Indian languages to the Indian recruits, especially the ladies.

Youth and Adult Training
The Manpower Services Commission (MSC) was the place. The Work Experience Programme (WEP) was the project we would be working on. Prime Minister Harold Wilson had suddenly realised that thousands of school leavers were hitting the job market with nothing to do. WEP was offering a financial incentive to companies to provide young people with genuine work experience covering workplace health and safety at work, and meaningful job skills experience. It would be a 26-week programme. Shortly after being at Selkirk House, Sir Richard O'Brien, MSC chairman, gave a press conference about WEP at the Construction Industry Training Board (CITB). Our immediate task on returning to the office was to answer questions on the telephone from interested parties: employers, parents, careers officers, young people, etc. We were a team of about five. No operational rules to follow. We had a clean slate. Fred Grafton, a former employment office manager and a few years from his retirement, was my line manager. He was a cool guy. He was always smiling. Nothing was ever an unsurmountable problem. He also had the experience of many years to call on in directing us as we set up the office. We read the info. I used my

correspondence course technique of underlying key points to good effect. We drafted introductory letters to local companies while the Head Office staff targeted the multinationals, local authorities, the Chambers of Commerce, and employer organisations. It was quick-fire action. Pressure was coming from the prime minister himself and so those below were even more frantic. It was chaotic, challenging, and fun.

Our staff number grew quickly. I was soon on temporary promotion to executive officer. I couldn't believe it. Jerry Brown surprised me by inviting me to accompany him to take part in an interview on Capital Radio. The WEP programme grew and thousands of young people benefitted from it. The office work was becoming a bit routine and I attended bookkeeping evening classes at Princeton College (now Westminster Kingsway College) for about two terms to help my understanding of accounts.

In July of 1977 I got married to Janice, a lady from the island of Montserrat, a legal secretary, who was a friend of one of my childhood friends. We met at our friend's home after being invited for dinner on Good Friday 1976.

Another training programme suddenly superseded WEP when in 1978, the Youth Opportunities Programme (YOP) was launched for 16- to 18 year olds. It required more-structured training. I was sent out to market the programme in addition to doing my normal office administrative work. One of the companies I went to was Schreiber Furniture. I met with one of the directors. His demeanour suggested he was probably expecting to see a white or older person. Not sure. I had prepared my presentation but was derailed when he said he had read the published information and had a few questions. I answered his questions to the best of my ability and hoped I would end up with some training placements. That wasn't the case. He did, however, write in to say that my presentation persuaded him to organize a larger intake of apprentices, nationwide. Yes, for that "achievement," I received a slap on the back, literally, from Fred Grafton.

My next move was to become the supervisor of the Marketing and Publicity Section. More money and more accountability was demanded. Sir Geoffrey Holland, (He was not knighted then but I'll use his title), was the MSC Director. He took a keen interest in the publicity side of things. I was among those present when a management consulting company was giving their presentation on their marketing strategy. It was ground-breaking because as far as I knew, the civil service hadn't previously allowed departments to indulge in advertising the way Sir Geoffrey planned to do. One of the consultants began to give examples of how advertising got a housewife to choose between brands of soap powder, even when there was little difference between them but for the packaging. At the end of the presentation, I opened my big mouth and asked how they thought that strategy would work when the programme was a voluntary one for young people and the choice facing them was a stark one of YOP or unemployment. There was stifled laughter by some and stony silence from others. One of the presenters began to elaborate on his strategy, speaking direct to Sir Geoffrey.
"What about what Roger said?" asked Sir Geoffrey. Before the presenter could answer, Sir Geoffrey asked the bulk of us to leave. Liz Hall, head of Marketing and Publicity and a handful of others stayed. The consultants came back about a week later. I wasn't invited to the presentation. Sometime later that day, somebody came and told me that Sir Geoffrey wanted me in the room where the presentation was being given. When I entered, they were discussing whose name would go on the press advertising as the contact person and one of the other guys' name was suggested. Sir Geoffrey wanted me to hear him say that I would be that person. That is how my name became nationally known. There were full-page ads in the national dailies and regional press about the YOP programme, and every one of them read: "For further information, contact Roger Panton," etc. on tel. no. xxxxxxxx" The funny thing

about that was that many people didn't think I existed. They thought it was a fictitious name.

In 1978, an adult programme, The Special Temporary Employment Programme (STEP), specifically for adults, joined the party. I was transferred from the Regional Office to the London Area Office. My specific role was to try and develop STEP programmes in the Borough of Hackney, highly populated by Black and Asian residents. It had exceedingly high unemployment. I would retain my temporary promotion. Alan Jones, the area manager, told me straight that he didn't want me there because he felt he had staff who could do the job. He said his hands were tied however, because it was a directive from the Regional Office. I had a desk with a telephone in a Council building in Old Street. I went out from there to discuss setting up STEP projects. One of the first projects was a community initiative set up by Charles Clark, later to become Home Secretary in Tony Blair's government (2004 – 2006). He was one of a small group of university graduates who moved into Hackney and worked tirelessly for the Labour Party. Stanley Clinton-Davis was the MP at the time.

It wasn't long before the Labour Government was under fire for not getting enough programmes underway and the Under Secretary in the Department of Employment, John Golding, MP for Newcastle-under-Lyme, paid a visit to Hackney. My area manager, Alan Jones, said I should be there. We met at the town hall and, after giving a speech about the importance of supporting the party's efforts to help their own residents, Mr. Golding began to criticize the MSC and the Council for not coming up with enough projects in the area. He was more severe in his criticism of the Council officers, berating them for lack of moral judgement in not looking after their own people. From Alan Jones's wry smile, he seemed happy that I appeared to be failing in my duty to generate many projects. I jumped in with an explanation to the Under Secretary. I didn't know that as a civil servant I shouldn't have done that. I had been introduced to him before, so he knew who I was. I explained that unlike his market town of Newcastle-under-Lyme, and other constituencies in the countryside, the officers of Hackney were not necessarily local. They came from all over the place so didn't have the local feeling and concern for kith and kin as he was suggesting. I knew what I was saying was fact because of my discussions with them. Several of the senior officers jumped in, appearing to relish the opportunity to support me. One by one they said they commuted from as far afield as Essex, Cambridgeshire, Hertfordshire, and Kent. Mr. Golding was wide-eyed, removing then replacing his wire-framed glasses repeatedly. He started to stammer as he vented his anger. He said how it wasn't supposed to be like that. Local government shouldn't be like that. It should be local. The officers should be local. Local government is for the local people to be governed by other local people. He added that they were probably being paid too much to be able to commute from so far afield. He felt the Council should follow the lead of the Metropolitan Councils and employ local people at 'officer' level, people who have a link with the community. He was furious. One of my colleagues told me later that I was lucky it turned out the way it did because Mr. Golding said he was glad for the explanation which I gave because it helped him to understand why the London boroughs operated differently from the countryside local authorities. Alan Jones never said a word to me.

Shortly afterwards, I left my special marketing role in Hackney and became a programme development and monitoring officer, in Alan Jones's London Area Office, still maintaining my temporary promotion to executive officer. It was a strange role in a way. I had to negotiate with providers to develop training programmes and followed that by monitoring the said programmes financially and qualitatively. The sort of things I unearthed included the use of a single voucher for two or more transactions; and the movement of large sums of money into a separate bank account immediately on receipt from the MSC, then back into the project bank account later, resulting in the theft of interest earned on the funds. As a monitoring officer I was elated to discover such wrongdoings and wanted the perpetrators brought to book, not just for the fraud but for thinking I was foolish enough to miss such things. What the public doesn't understand is that the role of the senior civil servant is to protect his/her minister from bad publicity, awkward questions in the House of Commons or from the Public Accounts Committee. Yes. That is so. A civil servant working "on the ground," so to speak, just wants to be efficient and gain promotion. But not making a big deal about the fraud becomes priority for the top folks. They're not condoning the fraudulent action by any means because action is taken – quietly. They just have different priorities. They can't go on record of telling a monitoring officer to cool things down a bit. What they do instead is to make the reporting of a suspected fraud the duty of an accountant a position that is more senior to that of the monitoring officer and more understanding of the need to protect the minister.

It was an exciting time for me because I was out and about on my own. Sometimes using my car, other times public transportation. I also helped in the training of new monitoring officers who would accompany me on visits to training programmes. The projects had a mixture of local authority, private sector, and community leadership. I worked with notable community organisations like NACRO (National Association for the Care and Resettlement of Offenders), and Community Service Volunteers. I sat on the interview panels for the recruitment of managers and accountants funded by the MSC. I enjoyed that aspect of the job. I also enjoyed the development meetings with local authorities, negotiating for training places. I also noticed that I was treated with a measure of respect that some of my colleagues complained about not getting. Most of the trainers, especially those based at the colleges, saw us as nothing more than pen-pushing civil servants. With me, however, they were mostly pleasant. I knew the tools and machinery they were using, and I could read some of the drawings. I was benefitting from my trainee toolmaker experience in my first job on arrival in London short though it was.

In one of my performance reviews with my line-manager Mark Wilkinson, one of the graduate entrants, he criticized me for being rude on the telephone to enquirers who sought information on setting up a project. He thought the word "no" was rude. I admitted that when callers gave me an outline of what they planned to do and asked me if that would be acceptable, I did say "no," if it warranted a negative response, but then I would go on to explain the ways the project could be tweaked to qualify for funding. He was not persuaded. What he thought I should have said was, "Not quite like that," then go on to give my tips on how the proposals could be shaped to qualify for funding. The "no" was a big deal for him. I refused to concede that saying "no" was rude. Not sure how, if at all, my refusal affected my report and therefore my career. I still think his view didn't make sense.

One of the things I learnt working in the arena of community project development is that the people in the community have brilliant ideas. Some of my colleagues behaved as if they knew it all and were not flexible enough when considering projects for funding. I remember when a group of women who met in an outbuilding of the Royal Artillery army barracks in Woolwich submitted a crèche project, our office manager, a former major and veteran of the Malaysian jungle warfare, described them as "Guardian-reading communists." (The Guardian is a left-leaning newspaper.) Crèche projects developed to become the norm later, with Gillian Shephard, Secretary of State for employment in Margaret Thatcher's government, launching in Docklands, with great fanfare, a national initiative for crèche provision. In addition, a couple of professors from Goldsmith College put forward a project to monitor pollution on one of the main thoroughfares on the outskirts of Lewisham. They were considered a bit weird because we didn't understand the implications of vehicle pollution. One only must look at the various legislations on pollution to see how vital that project was at the time.

Dealing with Black-sponsored project submissions wasn't easy for me at times. Many of the folks preferred to deal with my white colleagues because they could accuse them of racism if there was any difficulty with the projects getting approved. Because of this, I lift my hat off to Tony Suarez. He was with an organization that provided building renovation training for a group of young people in Wood Green, North London. Tony and I met at my office and he listened intently to what I had to say. He went away and re-shaped his submission. It was approved. Ujima went on to develop into a well-respected community organization.

There came a time when I received a telephone call from a friend, Tommy Tingling, a Jamaican, also ex-RAF. He was an executive officer (EO), working in the training section. Tommy asked me if I would be attending the current EO promotion panel. When I told him I was unaware of it, he asked me if I had been advised of the panel the previous year. I had not. I wrote to the Head Office human resource manager about both panels because I was qualified to attend both. I was then summoned to see Alan Jones. He just said it was an oversight by the human resource section and that I would be interviewed. When I tried to ask more about my omission, he simply said that it was water under the bridge. I had to agree with him. I went on the panel and was promoted, no longer being on temporary promotion. I was transferred to the Finance Section dealing with payments to the projects. Tommy introduced me to golf and he and I have remained friends and fierce competitors on the golf course.

In 1983, with Margaret Thatcher as prime minister, the Youth Training Scheme (YTS) replaced YOP. The training period remained at six months.

My 112 Squadron friend, Kieron, had moved from being a clerk to a become a commissioned officer and was a Squadron Leader at the Ministry of Defence. He'd also served at the Nottingham Careers Information Office, as Area Commander, after I'd left.

Kieron and I used to have lunch from time to time at the RAF Officers' Club in Piccadilly, at his invitation, of course. He retired as a Wing Commander. We've remained friends to this day, 53 years after we first met.

Small Firms and Regional Enterprise Units
The Department of Trade and Industry (DTI), is one of the oldest government departments and its officers consider themselves among the elites of the civil service, brokering business foreign and domestic, hobnobbing with the leaders of the international commercial world. They saw the Department of Employment as the lowly, to-be-kept-at-arm's-length job centre and benefits payment section, dealing with the unemployed. Without any prior announcement, the staff of the DTI's sections responsible for Small Firms and Tourism policy matters, along with the Small Firms Service, woke one morning in 1985 to find themselves in the Department of Employment, as part of Lord Young's responsibilities that was to be the Small Firms and Tourism Division. It was a present from Prime Minister Margaret Thatcher as she moved to enlarge the portfolio of Lord Young, the secretary of state for employment. Regional Enterprise Units (REUs) were the vehicles to deliver the domestic economic outcomes. Barry Horner, who I knew, but not very well, was appointed the head of the London REU. He made me a well-timed offer to join him and Ian Taylor in setting up the unit. I say well-timed, because I was on temporary promotion to higher executive officer at the time in the MSC Finance Section, streamlining the payment procedures for the adult and youth training schemes. Another EO had joined the section, and although he was less knowledgeable than me about the finance procedures, there was talk that we should at least share periods of temporary promotion by virtue of his EO seniority. The challenge of working with a blank sheet, as with the youth programmes, was so attractive, I couldn't let my temporary promotion hold me back. Going back to the lower pay at EO grade made my decision difficult. The challenge of the new job with a blank policy sheet, won. Not many, including my wife, thought my

move a wise one. That was who I was. I couldn't stop myself from taking up the intellectual challenges the new job posed for me.

My first few weeks were not at all comfortable listening to some of the DTI officers talk with disdain about the Department of Employment of which I had been a part for 10 years. Having said that, I could understand some of their points. There was an officer whose area included Cuba. He was angry that he wouldn't be getting his free cigars in Havana anymore as his main DTI colleagues would be dealing with the overseas issues. Also, many earned a fair amount of additional income through overseas travels. All was not lost for them though, because the DTI developed a policy to take back their favoured sons and daughters. They created jobs at a higher level than that which they held and brought them back on temporary promotion. For some reason, they couldn't go back on level transfer.

Setting up and helping to fund and develop enterprise agencies to assist in the development of small businesses, was a key task for us. Another was helping to remove barriers to small firms' development and to tourism, generally. A lot of that work centred on removing unnecessary bureaucracy. Organisations that were key partners included chambers of commerce; Business in the Community; LENTA (the London Enterprise Agency); the Royal Automobile Club (RAC); government departments like Environment, Transport, and Trade and Industry; the Metropolitan Police; and various employer associations.

When in Alan Jones' outfit, whenever I became the senior EO in a team and therefore in line for acting in my line manager's absence, I was moved to another team where I was not the senior EO. The result of that was I managed to work in nearly every London borough. As my new role in the REU involved all of London, I was able to call on contacts in nearly all the boroughs. There were benefits to being moved around, after all.

I remember a seminar we organized with the partner organisations. One comical situation that was unearthed involved traffic signs on the motorway. One could apply to the Department of Transport for permission to have an advertising sign placed by the roadside, advertising, say, a hotel. It could be denied because the Department of Transport ruled that the congestion of signs close to an exit from the motorway posed a safety hazard. The application could then be made to the Department of the Environment which would grant it if the sign were on the other side of the fence of the roadway. Each department was responsible for the area on one side of the roadside fence. There was no co-ordination between them. It was our task to try to remedy that sort of nonsense.

Another matter was the construction of the orbital London Motorway, the M25. The Croydon Chamber of Commerce and the RAC were vociferous in pressuring the Department of Transport to create a much longer exit lane from the M25 to both the M3, leading to Gatwick Airport, and the M4, leading to Heathrow Airport. The Department of Transport civil servants present at a meeting reeled off statistics relating to increased traffic forecast in the coming years and said the cost was not worth it then. I felt they gave the civil service a bad name. They didn't give the impression that they would consider the proposals, (which is what I think they should have done), but instead dismissed them outright. Extra lanes were created years later when the forecast congestions became dangerous as predicted by the RAC and the Croydon Chamber of Commerce. The parking of coaches in the West End at night-time and at weekends was a problem for the Westminster City Council. The coach operators were also seeking help for designated parking areas not too far from their drop-off points. The WCC's proposed remedy was for the police to enforce the parking restrictions that were on the books. The Metropolitan Police made it quite clear that they were not going to have their officers harassing coach drivers bringing elderly folks to a theatre performance when there was high crime to worry about. I suspect that this discussion led the Westminster City Council to start having traffic wardens. Other boroughs followed. I credit my boss, Barry Horner, with helping to boost my confidence yet further. He asked me to attend meetings on his behalf instead of cancelling them when other more urgent matters came up. His confidence in me was more than I'd expected at times and it helped me to manage difficult situations later in life. We've remained friends to this day. Our children, now around the 40-year mark, have formed their own close friendships.

In 1987, I was promoted to higher executive officer (HEO), the grade in which Flight Lieutenant Harry Friar had been when I joined the civil service, eleven years earlier.

CHAPTER NINE
Civil Service, Moving on

In 1987, my first job as a substantive HEO was with the Inner City Task Force. Once again, I was becoming involved with a new project – a blank sheet. Challenges galore to contribute towards developing a sensible operational policy. It was led by Ken Clark, minister of state for Employment. He was a cigar smoker and noted jazz aficionado. He wore light-coloured suits or sports jackets and, always, brown suede shoes. I liked him, (even though he was in the wrong party for me.)

The task forces were set up in eight small inner-city areas, experimenting with new projects and policies in Bristol, Birmingham, Manchester, and London. A particular aim of the initiative was to encourage job creation and enterprise, supporting small businesses, including those owned by ethnic minorities. High-quality vocational training was designed to improve the employment prospects of young inner city residents, mainly from ethnic minorities, and included finance, insurance, and hospitality industries. It was indeed a serious programme, targeted at specific areas, headed by a serious politician who liaised with the task force staff on all levels.

Soon after launching the task forces, Ken Clarke became minister of state for Trade and Industry. Instead of leaving the project behind for the incoming Employment minister, he decided to take us with him to the DTI. I wondered if he was aware of the contempt with which many of the former DTI Small Firms Service personnel held his Department of Employment and he was therefore spiting them by taking the task force to the DTI. The point is, we weren't really welcomed there, in their plush offices in Victoria Street. My previous roles were mostly at the sharp end, developing and monitoring projects. At the DTI, it was being the "link officer" between the task forces and the senior officers at the Head Office, gathering information and informing the task forces on policy development, visiting the task forces to get a feel for what they were doing, and editing reports coming in from them. The latter is something many didn't like. Though the heads of the task forces were two grades senior to me, some had poor grammar skills and their submissions couldn't really go further up the ladder without editing. I also drafted official replies for ministers who had to respond to their constituents on matters relating to the task force operations. This part of the job was something that my colleagues couldn't quite understand. How could I, not being a university graduate like they were, be employed on such tasks?

As the project expanded, it took on DTI staff. Everybody wanted to know my background. Usually, it was after they'd mentioned their degrees or the universities they'd studied at. I delighted in telling them I was a former RAF truck driver. Some, not wanting to define me by my truck-driving job, talked to me about other things they suspected I wasn't saying. Others were annoyed that a former truck driver, and from the from the Department of Employment as well, was doing the job I was doing.

After being in the DTI for just over a year, I was summoned to the task force director's office. Roger Knight, I think, was his name. He was someone I only saw at meetings or seminars. His secretary gave me a document and said the director wanted me to do a precis of it. I thought it a bit strange because there were two other officers in the management line between us and I'd never submitted anything directly to him before. But then, I also didn't know if my writings were passed on to him with my name on them, perhaps with amendments. I had a quick read of the first few lines then asked her what it was for. She said she didn't know and wondered why it mattered. I knew Mr. Knight was in his office and could hear our conversation. I told her that I did a journalism course and the amount of detail I would include in a piece would depend on what it was for. I told her the details would differ according to whether it was for local, regional, or national readership, so the purpose of the document mattered. She repeated she didn't know. I said, fine, and started walking away. She called me back and said I couldn't take the document away from the office. She then pointed to a desk with a notepad, already prepared for me. I thought: I wonder if Roger Knight wants to be sure the things I submit were really of my own doing? Anyway, I asked if I could use a highlighter and she said yes. I highlighted the main points, wrote my precis, and left. I never received a comment on it.

To ease the burden on himself, Mr. Clarke adopted a system of task force godfathers. These were government ministers whose roles were to be associated with a particular task force, visit selected projects, and meet with the local elected officials. One such godfather was John Cope, who took over Mr. Clarke's post of minister of state for Employment. I visited the Manchester task force with Mr. Cope. He asked me about where I was from originally, and he introduced religion into the conversation. He was delighted when he found I was, like himself, a Methodist, although he used the term "Wesleyan." A few months later, John Thompson, one of the senior managers, two grades above me, in the company of a man I'd not seen before, stopped by my office, and told me to come with him. They were going to see Minister Cope. That's all. No information as to why. After the greetings, we remained standing while Mr. Cope began to write with his fountain pen as both John and the other man dictated what turned out to be a speech about closing the Manchester task force. After the salutations, they got into more business-like statements, explaining how the task force had successfully achieved its objectives, and that they would be opening another one in another needy area.
"Come on. Let's have it," said Mr. Cope, looking up directly at me. I was a little startled by his somewhat crisp voice. Remembering how I'd spoken out of turn with Mr. Golding in Hackney, I

hesitated. "Let's have it. What's the matter?" he demanded. He had read my knitted brow and slightly open mouth well.

"Minister, it's just that earlier in the speech you gave the reason for closing the task force as because it had achieved its objectives. Now you're apologizing for closing it. It doesn't really…." I didn't complete the sentence.

"Quite," said Mr. Cope, looking up at the gentleman and my boss alternatively. He then angrily drew a line across the page, the nib of his fountain pen gathering paper as he did so. As he angrily cleared the paper from the nib, he said: "Right. Let's start again." Not a single word was said to me by my boss afterwards. I had about nine months to go at DTI and he never spoke to me again before I left. I was told by others that the other person was a researcher looking for a safe parliamentary seat and that I may have damaged his potential political career by my intervention. I don't know how my boss may have been affected by the said intervention.

When my time came to leave the task force, I had the option of returning to the Department of Employment or applying to stay in the DTI. They felt slighted when I dared to not even consider staying in their high-profile DTI.

CHAPTER TEN
Back in the Department of Employment

In 1990, I returned to the Department of Employment, sort of, to become the office manager of the London East Training and Enterprise Council (TEC), based in Aldgate. I say, 'sort of,' because the TECs were private limited companies in the process of taking over the roles of the Manpower Services Commission. They were going to manage various schemes including youth training apprenticeships. They also promoted training and business enterprise with local organisations.

The offices were mainly open plan, the trend of the day. I, as office manager, had my own enclosed office. Soon after I got there, that began to change as some of the other managers, some senior to me, didn't like the idea of me in my own enclosed office while they were in open plan. It wasn't too long before I lost my enclosed office, but I really didn't mind. It allowed me to be closer to my finance team of lovely, jolly, and mostly women from all over: Nigeria, India, the Caribbean and, of course, the UK. I was, for a time, in charge of purchases, including computers. I knew little about computers, but I was guided by others. My signature was, according to my job description, the authorizing signature for the purchases. When we were getting additional PCs, a supplier insisted on telephoning me at home, promising to give me a PC for my sons if only I'd give him the deal. First, it's the sort of dishonesty I couldn't contemplate. Second, I didn't trust this unknown person anyway. It could have been a setup. The authorizing signature responsibility was removed from me before the purchases could be done.

I was well into my second year when we started recruiting employees to work at the TEC, instead of using the civil service hiring process. The TECs and the civil service unions had been engaged in protracted negotiations concerning the employment and pension rights of those civil servants who chose to become TEC employees, and had finally reached agreement on pension rights. I had chosen to remain a civil servant because I didn't trust the TEC management. There seemed to be a clique that provided the top management, and if you were not a part of that clique, you wouldn't progress. I was a member of the interview panel for new office employees, but my management colleagues felt it wasn't right for me to be interviewing since I had shown no faith in the TEC management by electing to remain a civil servant. I was cool with that.

There was an incident that soured relations between me and the finance director who called me into her office to discuss a complaint by some of the young ladies on the finance team. Their complaint was that one of the men on the team, a bachelor in his late 40s, was standing much too close to them whenever they were talking. Moreover, he stared at them in a way that made them feel uncomfortable. The finance director told me I should be more observant of what was going on within my team and instructed me to have a word with the gentleman about his conduct. I told her I would speak first with Rupi, the supervisor of the finance team and take appropriate action following those discussions. She was not happy that I was not carrying out her instructions and she complained to the TEC director. After my discussions, I learnt that the ladies preferred to raise the matter with the finance director directly, as she was a woman, rather than with me. They'd feared a confrontation if I were involved. I didn't make a big thing of it. The gentleman explained that he was partially deaf, and he asked me to contact the civil service human resource department for confirmation because it's on his records. He said he stood close because he was lip reading as well as listening. That's all. Rupi and all the women saw the funny side of it and were satisfied all was well. They also had a good laugh about it. When I went to see my finance director, I noticed she had the phone slightly off the hook and I thought someone else might be listening to our conversation. I was super polite, and I told her that I was disappointed that someone at her level would instruct me to reprimand a member of staff without an investigation into the complaint being carried out. I then told her the result and she began to cry. I left the office. Nothing was said to me by anyone about that discussion.

Not too long after that, the TEC director, with my agreement, organised a secondment for me with Grand Met Trust, the subsidiary and training arm of Grand Metropolitan, the hotel and fast-food chain. The secondment would cover the last six months or so of my time with the TEC. Grand Met Trust had taken over the business training activities of a community project, Project Fullemploy, that was in operational difficulty. I spent some time learning about the Trust and working out a project solution that would suit both of us. This was necessary because the TEC seemed to want me to do work that would benefit them directly. That was fine. However, they wanted me to take my instructions from one of the TEC executive officers, one level below my own. I refused to work in that manner as I considered it a deliberate act on their part to belittle me.

One of the things the Trust was interested in was how the different enterprise agencies worked in the areas where both their organisation and the community projected operated. For Fullemploy, support for its trainees who were receiving financial assistance from the Department of Employment for small business training, was a priority. We agreed that I would visit enterprise agencies up and down the country and report on how they operated and how, if at all, the Trust could work with them to develop small businesses linked to business training. Having taken part in the setting up of enterprise agencies, it was interesting for me to be visiting them with a different eye. Some of the agencies I visited were not what I had envisaged an enterprise agency to be those years previously. They seemed geared to larger businesses and not the sort of place a fledgling entrepreneur would feel comfortable going to for assistance for his one- or two-person business. I also interviewed trainees, tutors and managers of the Trust's training projects. I was covering some old ground as I had done in the RAF and getting to know Britain even better than before. All the training and experiences I had accumulated over the years were coming together.

As I was about to leave the TEC and return to the Department of Employment, I had my performance review with the TEC director. In what I can only describe as revenge, he gave me a poor performance report. In my response, I addressed in writing all his detrimental comments, one by one, showing how wrong they were. I accused him of deliberately trying to damage my civil service career. I applied for and got a job with Acas, the Advisory, Conciliation and Arbitration Service, as a conciliator, dealing with employment disputes. I later heard that the board of directors to whom the report with my comments was forwarded (and perhaps due to the job I had moved to), dismissed the TEC director (or he resigned after a meeting with them).

CHAPTER ELEVEN
Acas, 1993

Acas aims to improve organisations and working life through better employment relations, working with employers and employees to solve problems and improve performance. Acas' role has developed considerably in recent years as arbitration and mediation have become more popular to reduce the number of cases requiring an employment tribunal hearing. The job of the conciliator was mainly to engage in telephone conversations with the disputing parties or their representatives to try and broker an agreement and avoid tribunal hearing. There was an option to hold joint meetings where the conciliator felt such a meeting could end with an early agreement. That was rarely used by my colleagues.

On arrival at Acas, I was surprised to find that I was the only Black conciliation officer there. I was immediately reminded of my days at Dakin Bros., as I listened to anti-Jewish comments by a particular Eastender. Often the comments followed his having a discussion with an employer. Part of the training involved listening to calls being made by the experienced conciliators. Not everybody was keen on my listening in on their calls. Still, they couldn't stop me if I chose to listen to a particular person's call. That's how the training was organized. Some were nervous of me. I really didn't know why. Still, I got by. Old habits die hard, though. Between 1976 and my arrival at Acas in 1993, I had specialized in developing new working procedures and contributing to policy development on a regular basis. Unfortunately, I took that habit with me to Acas and asked questions about things that had been done the same way for years without anyone thinking of a better way of doing them. I made enemies with my questions in the training sessions before I realized the harm I was doing to personal relationships with some of the "old timers." Yes. Questions. I had learnt years earlier that rather than make a statement that could hurt feelings easily, it was better, depending on the circumstances, to turn the statement into a question. The person to whom the question is posed, would get the drift.

I soon found that an extremely high number of Black people were involved with disputes and I was eager to get involved. I also knew that I had to remain impartial or I would easily get into trouble. I was, in fact, excited by the job of conciliator and I pushed myself to master employment law and disciplinary procedures as quickly as I could. I was able to use my RAF interview training to great effect in soliciting information from the parties. I decided early on to use joint meetings more, instead of protracted telephone calls over many months. My line manager wasn't keen on my doing so at first, as he feared I didn't have enough experience to be dealing with the lawyers who usually represented the employers and, occasionally, the employees. I persevered. I soon discovered that many of my colleagues who disliked joint meetings were lacking in confidence. They were more experienced than I and most had a better grasp of employment law and disciplinary procedures than I had. I wasn't ashamed to go into the meetings armed with a copy of the Disciplinary Procedure Handbook. They were simply scared of engaging in a face-to-face discussion with the lawyers and preferred the telephone, whereby the person at the other end couldn't see them leafing through the handbook or other material. Some of them treated the lawyers as some sort of demigods. This is not an exaggeration. I, on the other hand, relished the discussions with the lawyers even though I was one of the newer conciliators. Playing devil's advocate and putting doubt into each party's mind as to the potential success at a hearing – even if they won – was something I really enjoyed. I held joint meetings whenever I could and had a lot of success because I selected my cases for such meetings with great care.

One day, I was caught up in a dispute with a lawyer who accused me of not working in a timely fashion on one of his cases, causing him to have problems with his client. He cited speaking with me on a certain date and following it up with a letter the following day. My line manager Dave, took the attitude that appeasing the lawyer, come what may, was the thing to do. He did a draft letter for the assistant director, Ken Owen, to send to the lawyer. Ken sent it, copying me in. I did a note to Ken telling him that although I wasn't asking for anything more to be done with regards to the letter already sent, I wanted him to know that I didn't want the letter to be the last words on the matter. I drew his attention to the fact that both dates mentioned by the lawyer were prior to the employment tribunal sending out the papers. He simply said, ''Noted.'' Soon afterwards, I decided to apply to become a magistrate.

Magistrates in England and Wales do not need to be lawyers. Ken Owen had been a magistrate for some years. Instead of seeking permission from my line manager (as I would need for my court attendances), I went direct to Ken. He gladly approved and gave me some interview tips, adding that I should pop back to see him if I felt he could help me further. I was appointed as a magistrate in 2003. I knew that the civil service had a duty to support government policy relating to volunteering and decided to put as much time as possible into my attendance at court. I was therefore a regular at court, less than 15 minutes' drive from home. I couldn't see myself being promoted at Acas because there were too many HEOs who were more senior to me. It seemed that whenever they got to Acas they never left. I decided to plan for my intellectual challenges outside the civil service and as well as being a magistrate, I got involved with a variety of other voluntary activities: I chaired a school appeals panel, served as a charity trustee and school governor, helped senior secondary school students with interview technique and workplace health and safety training, and volunteered as a magistrate.

By 1995, Acas decided to experiment with "working from home" which was becoming fashionable. Long-serving conciliators could apply. To my surprise, many of the old timers had retired. Though not long-serving in civil service terms with just two years at Acas, I applied and was accepted on the pilot scheme. After the assessment of the pilot, Acas decided to discontinue the work-from-home experiment but gave members of the original pilot the choice of returning to the office or continuing to work remotely. I chose the latter.

Things were going well for me, working from home. My case load was monitored like all the other conciliators, which was not a problem. It was good for my golf, my family, and my health. I could get a few holes in at a nearby golf course early morning and late evenings in the summer. My sons, who were born in 1978 and 1980, benefitted from my being home when they arrived from school, as my wife was working in the West End. Not having to commute in crowded trains was also good for me. I had a big garden and was able to have short breaks tending my vegetables or simply tidying it. One day my line manager told me that if I were interested in promotion, I needed to work in the office so that, as the senior HEO on his team, I could substitute for him in his absence. I thought about the potential benefits of increased salary and pension based on final salary if promoted. But then, John Thompson, my former boss from the task force had become the human resource director at Acas Head Office. Oh well, I thought, rightly or wrongly, forget promotion. I decided to remain working from home. I was clearly not driven by money, and I wouldn't put myself in a position to be considered for promotion when I doubted, I would get it.

In 2005, I applied for early retirement and it was granted. My wife didn't think it a good idea for me to go it alone against the lawyers with my own human resource consultancy. My Acas colleagues also thought I wouldn't last. They couldn't see me surviving against the professional lawyers. From my experience as a conciliator, I was aware that I knew more employment law than many of the lawyers I had been dealing with. Many of my colleagues did also. I also had the confidence to challenge arguments in court. I had learnt a lot about court procedures from being a magistrate and, sitting on Magistrates' Court appeals at the Crown Court. The latter provided me with a tremendous learning forum. All that experience played a part in my decision to run my own consultancy.

Having read a lot about mediation, I decided that, with my joint meetings experience, I should be fine with mediation. I therefore went to see The Academy of Experts for more information and they agreed that what I did at joint meetings was akin to mediation. I took my annual leave and went on an Academy mediation course shortly before my departure from Acas.

CHAPTER TWELVE
Into the Lion's Den

After leaving Acas in 2005, my plan was to run my own human resource consultancy and include mediation as a service. My Acas colleagues believed I was walking into the lion's den. Sometime after leaving, the government decided to regulate the system whereby people who were not lawyers could charge a fee to employers and employees to handle their employment disputes. This was regulated by the Ministry of Justice under the Claims Management Regulations. I applied to become an "authorized person," and was approved. Heron Panton Consulting was born, but it wasn't as simple as I had thought it would be. In addition to liability insurance, we were forbidden to hold clients' funds without having an exceedingly high insurance policy for such funds. The thinking was that the Law Society covered lawyers who held the funds, so it made sense for us to have insurance cover to protect our clients. However, the cost was so high that I decided not to hold clients' funds and, of course, I had to make a statement to that effect. The policy for authorised persons was still in development and I was appointed a member to the consultative body, as a representative of authorised persons. That involved commenting on and contributing to the dialog concerning policy development.

An employment tribunal incident that remains in my memory is when I attended my first case management discussion. A case management discussion is an opportunity for the judge to determine what the issues are in a case and for the parties to agree a timetable for certain things to be done, e.g., disclosure of documents, exchange of witness statements, preparation of the trial bundle of documents, as well as the date of the hearing itself and how long it might last. I had sat through such discussions in the Magistrates' Court, but then we were mere spectators, as the defence lawyers and the Crown Prosecution Service put forward their plans and the clerk made notes. Although I read all the employment law books I could get hold of and was a member of an online library service whereby I could get copies of case law, I was more nervous at my first case management discussion than I had been at my first hearing representing an employer. The lawyer and the employment judge knew I wasn't a lawyer. The Queens Counsel or QC (an honorific accorded to barristers and solicitors of notable excellence and experience) who was representing the employer, had been speaking for a couple of minutes when the judge, staring at my knitted brow over his glasses, asked me what the matter was. I replied that I was a bit confused by what the QC was saying because he was stating what I had expected he, the judge, to say after he'd heard from both of us. The judge smiled and replied that I could rest assured that everything would be done by agreement. The QC apologized to the judge for getting ahead of himself. I was happy he went first, however, because although we had agreed beforehand on the issues in the case, I didn't have a good feel for how long it would take me to question his witnesses and how long the trial would last. I learnt a lot from the QC going first. The discussion turned out well and I was relieved. I had no idea I would've been so nervous about it.

The lawyers weren't happy with the arrangement for us non-lawyers competing with them and most of those I came across didn't enjoy dealing with me as their opponent. Some of them were hostile. Some were folks I had dealt with while I was at Acas, so they knew I had a good knowledge of employment law and disciplinary procedures. My weak point, in their eyes I thought, was my lack of training for the courtroom. Some of them didn't know what I had learnt from sitting as a magistrate; sitting at the Crown Court on appeals; and sitting as chairman of a school appeals panel, where lawyers often represented the parents. An important lesson I learnt being an employment tribunal advocate was to be always conscious that everybody has their first day on the job. That includes employment judges, and lawyers.

Most of my clients were Black employees, ranging from cleaners to a bank manager. On the other hand, my employer clients were mostly white and Greek Cypriots. I did a few of the employee cases free of cost because my costs would have taken up most of the financial remedy gained by the low-earning employees. As a friend told me, I was not born to be a businessman. The point is, having worked at Acas and seen how some of the employees gained extraordinarily little from their cases, I had no problem with it. I was also retired and on a pension. I did, however, take a couple of clients to the small claims court for non-payment because of their attitude towards me. One due to his deceit to me and to the tribunal, using false financial documents. The other, a lady who was angry with me for not allowing her to make serious, embarrassing, false allegations against an employer, in the hope of gaining a settlement.

I have a real appreciation for modern technology, even though I'm a bit slow to learn many aspects of it. Using my telephone, I was able to discuss with clients and charge for my time when I was in faraway places like Japan, New York, and California. I also had a telephone case management discussion with a judge and the other party when in New York. I built on the experience of my RAF interview training and included "independent interviewer" as a component of my consultancy. It gained me a few opportunities. They included a particularly good opportunity investigating a whistleblowing allegation, and two notable selection interview opportunities with the Home Office. The first was for a manager of a project, and the second involved selecting board members for the Metropolitan Police Complaints Authority (now the Mayor's Office for Police and Crime).

Parties in a commercial dispute before the courts may elect or may be guided by a judge, to take part in mediation to resolve the dispute. Mediation is cheaper and less time-consuming and less stressful than a court hearing. The parties are totally in charge when it comes to deciding the terms of the agreement reached. The mediator is, therefore, someone who is a good listener and who quickly recognizes and sets aside areas of agreement between the parties, thereby being able to get the parties to concentrate on the specific area of the conflict that needs resolving. Mediation also allows the parties to continue doing business together even during the resolution process. Court cases, on the other hand, are fiercer and usually mean the end of a working relationship. Unlike a court case that's a matter of public record, mediation is not. The terms of a mediated settlement are private. They can, however, become public if a party does not comply with the agreement and the aggrieved party seeks remedy through the courts.

At The Academy of Experts, I assisted in the training sessions of new mediators. I played the role of parties and their representatives. I also contributed to the discussions afterwards. I found that lawyers, in general, found the mediation process difficult. All their training is geared to their doing their best for their client. As a mediator, they don't have a client. They are supposed to be neutral. I found that in the main, after a short time, they gravitated towards one of the parties. I, however, understand that as mediation has become more popular, lawyers have become more adept at their impartial role. Mediation also provides opportunities to learn new things. Sometimes, it's a simple matter of the terminologies relating to the case. At other times, it can be information that boosts the mediator's confidence and impart that confidence to the parties. For example, if one had a case involving boats, it would help to know the difference between port and starboard, bow and stern.

Between 2006 and 2008, I had a spell of two years as an Academy of Experts "Member of Council" (a posh way of saying that I was a board member). I also wrote about mediation in The Academy's magazine and on my website and on social media platforms. I'm a strong believer in the mediation process and am pleased to see it's now a standard dispute resolution offering by Acas.

CHAPTER THIRTEEN
Outside Activities

In England and Wales, magistrates sit in groups of three, one of them serves as chairman, and the court clerk (a qualified barrister or solicitor) provides guidance on aspects of law and court procedure. The clerk is really in charge, despite how some chairmen pump up themselves. It wasn't long before I was in trouble with one of the clerks. In traffic cases where a person is disqualified from driving, the court clerk reads out a warning about the danger of flouting the law and driving while disqualified. The jurisdiction is also read out. I had noticed that they said the driving ban covered "Great Britain." New magistrates have a debriefing session after each sitting as part of the ongoing training. One day, I decided to ask a question that had been bothering me.

"Can a suspended driver drive in Northern Ireland?" I asked. The clerk quickly jumped in with an accusation that I was clearly not listening when in court and that she had said Great Britain. First, I thought it was a rude comment. Out of order, even. Second, she didn't seem to recognize that Great Britain did not include Northern Ireland.

"Can a suspended driver drive in Northern Ireland?" I repeated. She got red-faced and gave me a wicked stare. Marion, the chairman, a woman of many years' magistrates experience, interrupted.

"I sense that Mr. Panton is asking, if Northern Ireland is included in the ban, why isn't it mentioned?"

"Alternatively, why not say the United Kingdom?" I interjected. (There was really no need for my interjection, but I thought she was rude.)

The clerk seemed to be at the point of bursting into tears. The chairman turned to me and said, "Thank you Mr. Panton." I left the room. When my colleagues returned to the retiring room (where we all gather when not sitting in court), the chairman shrugged her shoulders and smiled. I later learnt that issuance of the warning is a specific role of the clerks and so the magistrates just never bothered to intervene. The clerks changed their statement because of my question. It was many months before I sat on a case with that clerk again.

As part of the training, magistrates are required to visit prisons. I visited Belmarsh, Holloway (now closed), and Feltham Young Offenders Institution (commonly called H M Prison Feltham).

Belmarsh, in South East London, is a Category A, modern prison with elaborate security systems. It housed prisoners with terrorism-related and other serious offences. We were taken to visit the Great Train Robber, Ronnie Biggs, who was housed in the medical wing. He could only communicate via an alphabet board but was in surprisingly good spirits. I'll never forget the banging and clanging that took place nonstop during the visit. I thought movies exaggerated that sort of thing. Believe me, it's real.

Holloway was said to be the largest women's prison in western Europe, until its closure in 2016. It was a depressive place. We met a small group of women, some with their babies.

Feltham Young Offenders Institution was the most depressing of all for me. The high number of Black youths in comparison to the total number incarcerated there was embarrassing. The booking-in process, which involved being stripped naked and being relieved of personal items, made me wonder about the mental state of those who were confined there. At the top of that system were "trusted offenders" who had the easiest of lives. They worked in the kitchens and catering stores and had generous access to snacks. I noticed one boy of mixed race. All the others were white or Asian. When we met with the deputy in charge (the heads always seem to have other appointments, even though the visits are arranged well in advance). I asked him how the "privileged" boys were selected.

He didn't like my question. He hesitated for a while, but eventually answered that they were selected by the wardens who could vouch for their good behaviour. I thought it sad that not a single Black youth was deemed to have behaved sufficiently well to warrant a place enjoyed by those we saw in the catering area.

An appeal against a magistrate's court decision is heard at the Crown Court. Two or four magistrates sit with the judge to hear the appeal. Each member of the bench has one vote when they retire to reach a decision. It's therefore easy for the judge to be outvoted on a decision. I was one of the magistrates who regularly sat at the Wood Green Crown Court with the judges. I was a civil servant and the government, as employer, must be seen to be supporting its own policy of volunteering. I was keen to observe and learn from the judges. I also paid particular attention to how the barristers would home in on one or two key issues, leaving out small matters that wouldn't make much of a difference to the case. That was problematic for many of their clients who wanted everything thrown in. I noted it for my employment tribunal cases. The court was providing me with a fantastic learning forum. After a few sittings, I asked some of my more-experienced magistrate colleagues about the practice of our sitting with the judges. To be honest, I couldn't understand why we needed to be there because the judges were in full control and I couldn't see what we were adding to the process, except for numbers on the bench. My colleagues reaffirmed that because magistrates dealt daily with the cases that were appealed, the judiciary felt it wise for them to take part in the appeals process. As beneficial as it was for me on a personal basis, I noticed from unsolicited comments made by some of my colleagues (for my benefit, I thought), that they didn't think it good practice to overturn the decisions of "our magistrate colleagues." I was uncomfortable with that as I felt that that attitude was interfering with justice. I therefore made my feelings known to them. I thought how magistrates participate in the appeals process was something the Ministry of Justice should look at. I didn't think the judges would miss the magistrates and that justice would still be done. I resigned at the end of 2011 and gave up my consultancy in 2012, months before my 70th birthday.

I became a member of the Edmonton Labour Party in 1978 until I went off on my travels after retirement. Ted Graham was our MP at the time, Andrew Love, at the end. Being a civil servant, I didn't get involved with too many activities although I manned the telephones sometimes at election time, trying to get voters out to the polls. One of the things I noticed was that although general meetings were sparsely attended, when it came to the AGM, it was the time for people to come out of the shadows and be nominated and seconded with great speed for all sorts of positions. The organization among them was impressive for that sort of thing. I was at first surprised by it, but in time, I understood 'the workings.'

While a member of the Parents' Association Committee of one of my sons' secondary school, three vacancies arose for governors (school board members). My committee colleagues who had already had their private discussion, approached me to apply for one of the vacancies which would be awarded by a vote of the parents. I told them that I didn't know enough parents to win a place. They told me all I needed to do was fill out the application and leave the parents to them. There were five competitors for three places, and I won one of the places. One piece of information that I think helped me was that I was already a volunteer, monitoring the school's work experience placements for the 6th formers.

The school was just starting a new management structure of moving from under the control of the local education authority to being an independent company, a grant-maintained school, managing its £3.2-million budget. It was a very new responsibility for the long-serving governors. Governors who were "old boys" of the school, seemed to take some time to recognize that they were, in fact, directors, with all the legal responsibilities that entailed. Whenever key issues were raised, the initial comment was, "I think I know an Old Boy who might be able to help." The chairman was from the Education Authority and my colleagues, in the main, continued to look to the Authority for policy guidance. I soon had differences of opinion with some of them. As a "New Boy," and perhaps a Black one at that, that wasn't supposed to happen.

An area of annoyance was that they habitually singled out the Black boys in the student body for criticism relating to bad behaviour. I accept there was bad behaviour among some of them. At the end of my first year, however, the statistics showed white English boys among the worst behaved. I listened to their criticisms again before drawing their attention the stats and asking them how those criticisms squared with the stats in front of them. Eerie silence. That's how they dealt with things they couldn't defend: silence. I also found that putting forward ideas had its own problems. Calling on my varied experience, I did that from time to time. They had a strategy whereby one of the Old Boys would repeat what I had said with a variation or two. The minutes of the meeting would then credit them with the idea, and I wouldn't get a mention. I considered it a conspiracy, but it didn't stop me because others were noticing it and the benefit to the school was paramount. After all, one of my sons was a student there.

I was on the interviewing panel to appoint a new head of school. There came a point when the choice was between one of the deputy heads and an outside candidate. The final vote was 3 to 2 or 4 to 3 (I can't quite remember), in favour of the outside candidate. A bad move on my part it seemed, because the chairman and I were in the majority in opposition to the Old Boys on the panel, when we voted to appoint the outside candidate. Later, when it was time to select a new chairman, the front runner was the female human resource director of a local company. Prior to the meeting, some of the Old Boys on the board, made it clear, that there was no way they would serve under a woman as chair of the board of governors of their boys' school. They'd resign if a woman were elected. A former head, who was also a governor, and others, approached me to put myself forward for the position of chairman, assuring me of their support. I declined. I resigned after serving for two years.

As chairman of the Enfield Grammar School Disciplinary Appeal Panel, I was subjected to an interview by the school district ombudsman, following an appeal to the ombudsman by a parent who challenged a decision we reached to exclude her son from the school. The ombudsman ruled that we had acted properly within the law and the procedures. Following the ruling, the Enfield Education Authority lawyer in charge of the school appeals process asked me to become a member of the School Appeals Panels, run by the Education Authority for all its schools. The role of the independent panel was to decide whether a child who had been refused a place in a school of their choice, should be given a place upon appeal. The panel also determined whether a child had been properly excluded from school on account of failing to comply with disciplinary requirements, or where the pupil's continued attendance at the school was likely to be seriously detrimental to order and discipline or to the educational well-being of the other pupils. Soon after joining the panel, I was elected a chairman. I added the Education Act to my list of legal knowledge of employment law and criminal law. I served on the panel for 17 years.

One case that stands out in my mind relates to how a church school manipulated the admissions rules to deny entry to siblings. As panel members, we couldn't challenge a schools' admission policy if it were properly constituted and published within a certain period before applications for entry to the school were made. (This was the government policy at the time). This church school had experienced falling rolls a few years earlier and, to stop the drain and possibly face closure, it changed its admissions policy to include a wider catchment area where many Black people lived. The siblings rule gave priority to new applicants who had a sibling already at the school. As a result, they had an influx of Christian African pupils who were members of large families. After a while, this meant too many African pupils for their liking. The school then reversed its policy, shrinking the catchment area and getting rid of the siblings' priority rule. One of my long-serving white panel colleagues, who was aware of when the previous policy had been instituted, was truly angry with the school representative at the hearing. It was out of character for him to be so angry, but there was nothing we could have done, because the policy was properly constituted.

It was daunting for some parents to appear before the panels and I thought that having more Black panel members might ease their anxieties. Although I managed to get a few members of the Black community to serve on panels, there were not as many as I would have liked. I hoped this would change. A common appeal was where a sibling was refused entry to a school under a "sibling rule" (one of the priority headings for entry). Despite information available to parents, many seemed to overlook the fact that having a sibling in the 6th form did not trigger the sibling rule, as 6th form entry was by invitation and did not fall under the provision of compulsory education. (At least, that was the case when I was there.)

Barnet Education Business Partnership aimed to improve the link between schools and the business world. My role, via my consultancy, was to help prepare the senior pupils with interview technique, and workplace health and safety training. I soon found that I was, at the time, the only Black volunteer with the title "business." It was as if Black people didn't do business. I did this for about four years.

Following an invitation from one of my magistrate colleagues who was also a local councillor, I became a board member of Enfield Enterprise Agency, established in 1985 and still going strong as I write. It's one of the first enterprise agencies we set up in the TEC programme, and two of the original staff were still there when I joined the board. One was the director/board member (his wife was the person objected to by the Enfield Grammar School Old Boys), and the other, the manager.

CHAPTER FOURTEEN
Spain and Other Travels

Following hurricane Hugo that devastated the island of Montserrat in 1989, I became a founder member and trustee of a charity called MAC89 (Montserrat Aid Committee 89). Montserrat is a British Overseas Territory. We raised funds to assist the islanders recover from their losses. In 1995, Montserrat's volcano erupted and MAC89 became the main engine to lobby the UK government and businesses for help. Dust masks were provided by 3M (UK), and medical supplies by Boots, the Chemists. Our lobbying led to the islanders being granted UK residency. They therefore became eligible for government assistance that would be appropriate in the circumstances. One of my roles, which Acas was aware of and gave me time off to deal with, was to accompany financial benefit seekers to appeal hearings after their applications were denied. I was also responsible for settling children into schools all over England. I received calls of thanks for quite some time from parents after some of the children were placed. My ex-wife, also a founder-member of MAC89 and who is from Montserrat, became the island's UK representative.

My older son Stuart, who did a physics and business management degree at the University of Manchester, is married, and has two sons. He's a physics teacher in London. He's partly responsible for my voluntary activities. When he was 8 or 9 years old, he asked me why all the policemen, nurses, firemen and others who visited his school to talk to them were white. I tried my best to deal with it by pointing out that it was either the choice of the teachers who invited them, or who the organisations chose to send, as there are Black people in all the professions he mentioned. I have never forgotten that question. My other son Kevin, who is single and studied English and philosophy at Keele University, has moved to Portugal where he does home tutoring. He previously juggled teaching at a Steiner School with running poetry workshops and being a rapper.

My wife and I filed our divorce papers in late 2012, after having lived separate lives, having no dependent children, and sorting out our finances and property ourselves. Just before Christmas 2012, I headed to Malaga, Spain. Golf for the next few years was the plan.

In deciding where to stay in the province of Malaga, I contacted my sister Beverley and her husband Dave. They had an apartment not far from Fuengirola where they spent periods of time each year. I checked out accommodation and settled on the Aparthotel Myramar. It was a hotel that catered for people who wanted to stay for long or short periods. It had cooking facilities but provided the normal daily hotel services as well. I chose to have breakfast and evening meal. The choices were very varied with fresh salads, vegetables, and seafood. That was fine for me.

Beverley and Dave were friends with a Jamaican golfer, Arthur, who lived in Fuengirola. We met. I joined the El Chaparral Golf Club where he was a member. It was quite an international outfit with members from all over the world. In addition to Spain itself, members came from Britain, Cuba, Denmark, Finland, France, Germany, Ireland, Norway, Peru, South Korea, Russia, Sweden, and Switzerland. Some were residents of Spain, others were, like me, long-term stayers. We had regular competitions, playing up to five times a week sometimes. It was a matter of getting to the club by 9 a.m., playing golf, and then spending time on the terrace afterwards. That could take up six hours easily, especially when the "pay-out" to the competition winners couldn't be made until the last golfers were in. I enjoyed my time at the club, making new friends and playing in competitions for El Chaparral against other clubs in the area. I also joined friends from the ACGA (African

Caribbean Golf Association), a UK golfing organization of which I'm a former Secretary, in a golf competition when they visited. Most of the guests I got to know in the hotel were pensioners from the northern countries of Europe, spending three to six months starting in October or November each year, to avoid the winter cold of their homelands. The short-term stayers also included many visitors from inland Spain, as well as Moroccans who came over for lavish weddings and shopping sprees. The winter stayers helped the hotel to stay open in the winter off-season and earn from other services that included conference facilities for the police and other organisations. One morning, the manager told me he lost several guests who decided to move out early when a group of uniformed police officers arrived for a seminar.

The hotel was next to a shopping centre with a bus terminal from which one could travel along the main coast road from Malaga to Marabella and beyond, and all the essential amenities to make one feel comfortable: shops, food store, cafes, restaurants, and cinema. I didn't need to own a car but would hire one whenever I needed to. I also became friends with the front desk staff and the management, in general. They were interested in my writing and gave me ideas for my third book. I made friends with many of the hotel guests as well. My son Stuart also stayed there with his wife and the first of his two sons.

Over the years, I was lucky to have travelled a bit in addition to my RAF service. As a family, we went to Montserrat, Jamaica, Spain, and the US. On my 60th birthday in 2003, my wife and I went on a Caribbean cruise and visited several islands. Other trips took us to Cuba, Switzerland, and Italy, visiting the typical tourist attractions. I thought of my Latin teacher, Mrs. Parkins, all the time when in Italy, especially when I stood by the sign indicating The Appian Way, near an ancient wall.

In 2007, on my way back from my son Stuart's wedding to Maiko in Kagoshima, Japan, I left from Narita airport, the airport I had read so much about years earlier. Stuart had quit high-pressure city banking and gone to Japan to teach English and further his martial arts studies. He spent five years there. While in Kagoshima, I visited Miyazaki, where bustling modern city life co-existed side by side with areas of narrow streets and tiny traditional Japanese houses. I later told Maiko that I noticed at the airport, uniformed young ladies running beside passengers with the passengers' hand luggage, many of the passengers being males, and wondered why they did it. Her response was, "In England, don't they care whether their customers catch their flights?"

The Cuba holiday was in the resort of Varadero, east of Havana. I learnt to scuba-dive in a pool and had to pass a test before being allowed to go diving at the Bay of Pigs. Part of the test was being able to remove the mask and put it back on safely, under water, expelling the water from it. When we went to collect our diving kit, my instructor and I were standing together chatting in Spanish. I noticed some of the staff looking at us and whispering. My instructor went over to them, chatted, and laughed before returning. He explained that because of the way I was standing, erect, arms folded and appearing to scrutinize what was going on and speaking in Spanish with him, the staff thought I was a military man, probably a health and safety inspector. The consequence of that was that they slowed down the issue of the equipment, taking care to follow the checking procedure, item by item customer by customer, rather than say, issuing them in bulk to each person. The military was still with me, it seemed. I also had a day trip to Havana. It was an exceptionally long bus ride. Things were organized for us. We visited tourist locations like the Che Guevara monument, the sea front, old Havana, and Ernest Hemingway' house. At night, we went to two large hotel rooms: one each for the men and women, where we showered and changed. We also took in the cabaret show at the Tropicana Night Club, a colourful spectacle of Cuban music and dance.

I had many visits to the US, mostly to New York. I played golf there and in the UK with my brother Deryck, who I miss dearly. He succumbed to cancer in 2011 on our parents' wedding anniversary. I also spent three months in Los Angeles, taking in Christmas 2015. I stayed with my goddaughter and family. It was a fantastic holiday. I met some interesting and fun guys who became regular golfing friends taking me to golf courses all over LA. Through them, on different occasions, I met Smokey Robinson of Mowtown fame, and Jim Brown, the actor and Hall of Fame Cleveland Browns running back. Smokey was a decent golfer and extremely sharp dresser on the course, outfitted in red and black. Jim was an excellent golfer. What surprised me was that they both played on public courses instead of at private clubs. I later chastised myself for being surprised. They were clearly happy playing with the local folks at Encino who treated them as just one of the regulars. No fuss. They didn't bargain for me having to have my picture taken with them. They were accommodating, perhaps my being a visitor.

I published my first book, *Mr. Alexander*, in 2011. It was an expanded short story that I tried to get published as such a few years before. It was published first in hardcover and later paperback but is now only available via Amazon Kindle. A reader of *Mr. Alexander*, thinking it was a true story, asked me to write her true story of abuse by her mother from about the age of three. After a couple of meetings and reading newspaper reports about her in later life, of which she was rightly proud, I presented her with an outline of the story. She changed her mind, saying she felt her younger sisters would be identified through the story. The problem for me was that the idea of childhood abuse wouldn't leave my head. I went back to her with my idea for a fiction on child abuse and she agreed it was nothing like her story, so she was happy for me to go ahead with my story. *Daisy McIntosh*, published in 2014, became my second book. My third book had a more light-hearted beginning, and that is reflected in the story. The hotel front desk staff had given me a few ideas for it, and I was thinking about them.

Then, at the Valentine's Day party being held at the hotel in 2015, I was chatting with them when we saw a young man was pacing across the hotel entrance, after all the young lovers had been called into the restaurant. He took strong puffs on his cigarette with each step. A call on his cell phone interrupted his routine. He crushed the cigarette with his shoe and dashed into the hotel and asked the whereabouts of a hotel with a similar name to the Myramar. They told him it was about 10 minutes' drive away and gave him the directions. He ran out of the hotel. That, I told them, would be the story of my next book. I changed the location to London, and the occasion to millennium night. That's how *Gina Johnson* became my third book. I'm still in touch with some of the staff, although the hotel is closed because of the Covid-19 virus.

CHAPTER FIFTEEN
Back to where it all started

I left Spain in May 2017, spent two months in London, then came to Jamaica in July, with a plan to return to Spain via London, in October. Sometime in August, Thandi Pryce, a teacher at Fair Prospect Primary school, asked me to help her prepare some Spanish lessons. The government had decided to introduce Spanish in the curriculum of the primary schools, but there weren't enough Spanish teachers to make it happen. After some discussion, I decided to postpone my return to Spain and teach at the school – on a voluntary basis – for a while. I ended up volunteering at three local primary schools (well, I did get a free lunch and water). On Mondays, Tuesdays, and Thursdays, respectively, I taught at Fair Prospect, Rural Hill and Manchioneal (my old school). The Covid-19 epidemic put a stop to my teaching in March 2020.

In addition to the teaching, I was the vice chair of UK charity EPOCC (Ellen Pearl Outreach Children's Charity), started by a friend, Beverley Chung. We raised funds in the UK to set up a project to provide in Jamaica a free telephone counselling service for young people who were being abused or under threat of abuse, or who just wanted to talk to a trained counsellor about any subject of concern to them. It was modelled after Childline UK. Being in Jamaica, I became the head of the operation there – Childline Jamaica. Unfortunately, despite the involvement of the Child Protection and Families Services Agency, the Office of Utility Regulators (for the toll-free line), the police, and the telecom companies Flow and Digicel, Covid-19 was just one hurdle too many for EPOCC to overcome. The project had to be abandoned.

My stay here in Jamaica was not planned but I'm incredibly happy to have decided to stay on to help the children who are mostly keen and quick to learn. Walking through the district and hearing them greet me in Spanish is music to me ears. Hearing the older ones read six- and seven-figure numbers off the board in Spanish is sheer joy. Watching them grasp the grammar when some Cuban teachers I met thought it was a bridge too far, is unforgettable. Being told off by 7 and 8 year olds who hear me greet a teacher in English instead of Spanish is so touching. Teaching Spanish in my old age is something I'm quite content with and I'm hoping Covid-19 will allow me to continue doing so sometime soon. I'd just like to add this: we really do need to have more male teachers in Jamaica and England. Our young children need to have them around in a supportive role within the school setting.

I've been in touch with some of my Happy Grovian classmates: Cynthia Perkins, Dorothy Neufville, Margaurite Mongol, Ranford Ramdatt (the names "of old"). I'm sadden by the death of Astley Burrowes and Jack DeLisser in early 2020. I told you earlier, about Burrowes. DeLisser, another boarder, came to Happy Grove three years or so after us. He was quite an athlete. Since my return to Jamaica, we met a few times in Kingston for lunch and had lots of telephone conversations between 2018 and early 2020. Also, in 2020, I managed to put cousins in Cuba in touch with each other. My late Uncle Eli and late Aunt Evelyn (brother and sister to my father), both have descendants in Havana and other provinces, but neither family was aware of the other. I was in touch with my cousins from Aunt Evelyn and was recently put in touch with my cousins from Uncle Eli. In November 2020, and again in December 2020, they got together at a birthday party in Havana. They're all tremendously happy about getting to know each other and more family get-togethers are planned.

I recognize that my road has not been a smooth, well-planned one. I started my educational path with gusto with many hidden dreams. The deviations were at times sudden and the alternative pathways rocky and uneven. My decisions appeared impulsive at times. However, I always believed that whatever obstacles lay ahead, I was equipped to overcome them. Some may consider some of my decisions foolhardy. For me, I always felt that, as with walking, each step would take me closer to a destination that would be a good one, even if at the time I didn't have a clue where that destination lay. I recognize that I couldn't have succeeded and had so much fun with the challenges if I didn't possess the feeling that all would be well. Confidence in myself was, I think, a key element. Some people, when in a dissatisfied situation say, "opportunity will knock for me one day." The question is, what preparation is there to first, recognize the opportunity when it arrives and, second, be equipped to make use of it? I think I did my bit to prepare and was fortunate to have had folks who recognised I had the ability to perform certain tasks despite my lack of formal qualifications as proof that I was capable. They gave me the chance to make or break. I'm grateful to all of them. I tried to instil in my sons the importance of taking the opportunities that come their way. I've spoken to them about my own path and am pleased that they don't have to walk the path I've walked. My path was special for me, for my personality. A friend commended me on my voluntary activities, but I think my indulgence was aided by Stuart's question about the lack of visible Black professionals when he was at primary school. I do however believe that I'm wired to act in the way I did. Not answering the various calls to action would have been more difficult.

Despite what I consider to be my successes, I still didn't manage to achieve two important goals I set myself at different times and there's no hope now of my ever achieving them. First, I've never scored a century in cricket, 87 being my highest score, achieved on the hard wickets in Cyprus. Second, I never quite made it to being a single-figure handicap golfer, 11 being my lowest. I still try to improve myself in other areas, including improving my Spanish. I watch a YouTube Latin American daily broadcast of civil court proceedings called *Caso Cerrado* (Case Closed). I might well be seen by some as being obsessive about the language, but I'm content, especially when I see how others have benefitted from it.

I'm pleased that despite the hurdles I faced in trying to "catch up" on what I consider a great educational start in my young life, I never lost heart. My somewhat haphazard journey, although for the most part challenging and interesting, was also a lot of fun.

...END...

Printed in Great Britain
by Amazon